THE LORD OF THE NEW COVENANT

Bishop Charles L. Middleton, Sr.

The Lord of the New Covenant
New Foundations Study Course Section Two
ISBN: 978-1-946180-10-0
Copyright © 2003 by Charles L. Middleton, Sr.
Charles L. Middleton Ministries, L.L.C.
8220 Second Avenue
Detroit, Michigan 48202

Published by
Covenant Outreach Publishing, Inc.
Detroit, Michigan

Cover and Text Design: Lisa Simpson
www.SimpsonProductions.net

This is The Christ

James E. Faust and Jan Pinborough

They heard His voice, a voice so mild;
It pierced them through and made their souls to quake;
They saw Him come, a man in white,
The Savior who had suffered for their sake.
They felt the wounds in hands and side,
And each could testify:

This is the Christ, the holy Son of God,
Our Savior, Lord, Redeemer of mankind.
This is the Christ, the healer of our souls
Who ransomed us with love divine.

I read His words, the words He prayed
While bearing sorrow in Gethsemane;
I feel His love, the price He paid
How many drops of blood were spilled for me?
With saints of old in joyful cry
I too can testify:

This is the Christ, the holy Son of God,
Our Savior, Lord, Redeemer of mankind.
This is the Christ, the healer of our souls
Who ransomed us with purest love divine.

ACKNOWLEDGEMENT

I want to acknowledge here the special gift from Dr. Sam Storms to this writing project. Sam is the lead Pastor of Bridgeway church in Oklahoma City, and he serves on the board of Bethlehem College and Seminary. The two main articles in the appendix **[Is the New Covenant for Israel or The Church?"**, and **"The Surpassing Glory of the New Covenant:]** were written by Pastor Sam Storms. These blogs reflect a perspective that deserves our upmost attention. I highly recommend his book, "Kingdom Come" as a worthy resource for all serious students of Biblical Eschatology. Thank you, Pastor Storms for your timely investment and partnership in the business of the Father.

CONTENTS

PREFACE

Who God is, and what it means to be divine, is something that we can only learn at the place where God reveals it. That place is Jesus Christ. Again, who we are, and what it means to be the covenant partners and friends of God, is something that we alone can learn at the place where God reveals it. That place, again, is Jesus Christ.

These opening statements grow out of the conviction that the Lord Jesus Christ is *the* key to understanding **God, the Bible,** and **the New Covenant Life** into which we've been placed. He is the fulfillment of the Old Testament types and prophecies; plus, He is the thematic unity of the entire span of Biblical revelation.[1] Obviously, anyone with such far reaching importance deserves our utmost attention.

The apostles of old taught that, "In the past, at various times and in various ways, God spoke to the fathers by the prophets. In these last days, however, He has spoken to **us** by His Son — The Lord Jesus Christ" (Heb. 1:1 ff.). The Lord Jesus Christ is therefore the indisputable center of the salvation history which the Old Testament describes, and the New Testament fulfills. Here, in this special stream of events God has **acted**, and **spoken**, and **"presented Himself."** That's why we call Jesus "Immanuel" or "God with us." He is "God expressed." The beloved apostle John referred to him as "The Word Made Flesh" (Jn. 1:14) and in so doing he ascribes ultimate value to a Hamitic Jew from Nazareth who was born of a young African girl

---

[1] Norman L. Geisler, **Christ: The Key to Interpreting The Bible** (Chicago, Moody Press, 1968), p. 7

of marriageable age. Again, the saving activity of God in the history of mankind came to its most definitive expression in the person and work of Jesus Christ, the Nazarene. And, the redeemed community of disciples, that we call the church, is his creation and his authorized, visible representative in the earth today.

This small book is all about what the Christian churches, historically, have always believed about their Lord. The entire revelation of Scripture is called upon throughout this study; but, special emphasis has been placed upon New Testament Truth. Our conviction is that the Old Testament must be read in light of the New Testament because that is the light in which our redemption and destiny is seen in its clearest form. The insights given into the creeds, and what they teach us about the Atonement, Redemption, Propitiation and Reconciliation are priceless; moreover, I believe that you will experience a tremendous "boost-in-the-spirit" by daily affirming the benefits that have been provided for us by the Lord Jesus Christ in His atoning work on the cross.

Finally, I am pleased to present, for your edification, "the Ligonier Statement on Christology." This concise affirmation of faith is one of the things that binds us all together in that sacred community called "the church." You would again do well to confess this statement everyday — affirming its truth out loud. In this way, truth that initially resides in your head will come to reside in your heart, where from "the issues of life" spring forth (Prov. 4:23).

The Word Made Flesh
The LIGONIER
STATEMENT
On CHRISTOLOGY

We confess the mystery and wonder
    Of God made flesh
    And rejoice in our great salvation
    Through Jesus Christ our Lord.

With the Father and the Holy Spirit,
    The Son created all things,
    Sustains all things,
    And makes all things new.
    Truly God,
    He became truly man,
    Two natures in one person.

He was born of the Virgin Mary
    And lived among us.
    Crucified, dead, and buried,
    He rose on the third day
    Ascended to heaven,
    and will come again
    In glory and judgment.

For us,
    He kept the Law,
    atoned for sin,

and satisfied God's wrath.
He took our filthy rags
and gave us
His righteous robe.

He is our Prophet, Priest, and King,
Building His church,
Interceding for us,
And reigning over things.

Jesus Christ is Lord;
We praise His holy Name forever.
Amen.

1

"THE NEW COVENANT"

Though the prophets of Israel and Judah lived under the Mosaic covenant, they were enabled by the Holy Spirit to prophesy about the New Covenant. Jeremiah gave the clearest and fullest message concerning the New Covenant that the Lord said he would make with the House of Judah and the House of Israel in the last days. What he had to say about this covenant actually set the stage for the New Testament revelation of the person and work of Jesus Christ. The late Donald C. Stamps commenting on this subject, observed the following:

> "Though Israel and Judah repeatedly broke God's covenants, and were subsequently broken in judgment for their backslidings, Jeremiah prophesied about a day when God would make a New Covenant and turn things around."

Stamps goes on to say, a major albeit unpopular truth that we must always affirm: He says,

> **"The New Testament makes it clear that this New Covenant was instituted with the death and resurrection of Christ (Luke 22:20; cf. Mt. 26:26; Mk. 14:22-25) and is now being fulfilled in the church—the New Covenant people**

of God (Heb. 8:8-13). This covenant will climax in the end-time salvation of the nation of Israel (Rom. 11:27)."

This is very key! The church (not Israel) now constitutes the New Covenant people of God.

On the night before His death, while celebrating the Passover with His disciples, the following scene occurred:

> **²⁶ And as they were eating, Jesus took bread, blessed and broke it, and gave it to the disciples and said, "Take, eat; this is My body."**
>
> **²⁷ Then He took the cup, and gave thanks, and gave it to them, saying,**
>
> **"Drink from it, all of you,**
>
> **²⁸ For this is My blood of the new covenant, which is shed for many for the remission of sins."**
>
> **Matthew 26:26-28 NKJV**

Essentially, this covenant is the new relationship with God that was spoken of by Jeremiah and Ezekiel (Jer. 31:31-34; 32:27-44; 50:4f; Ezk. 37:15-28). Jesus used the occasion of the Passover to gather and to address the nucleus of the New Nation (the Church) that was to replace the old Nation of Israel (Mt. 21:43; I Pet. 2:9-10). In this historic moment, Jesus changed the meaning of the elements of the Passover meal and established a bond that would fulfill all of the earlier covenants from Adam to David.

THE REALITIES OF THE NEW COVENANT

The prophet Ezekiel (following along in the same stream as Jeremiah) tells us that, under the New Covenant, God is going to cleanse us from our filthiness; put a new heart or spirit within us; and fill our new spirit with His very own Holy Spirit (Ezek. 36:25-27). All of this comes as a gift to everyone who believes in the Lord Jesus Christ. Moreover, in the power of His grace, we will be enabled to love and to obey God spontaneously (Ezek. 11:19-20).

The New Covenant is further characterized by the following additional realities. First of all, there is the reality of Divine healing, miracles and gifts (Mk. 16:15-20; Acts 4; I Cor. 12:1-12; Jas. 5:14-16). Secondly, there is the reality of deliverance from demonic oppression (Lk. 13:10-17). It is interesting to note here that, Jesus used this reality as a positive sign that the Kingdom of God had indeed drawn near to men. The final reality is the reality of redemption from the curse of the law (Gal. 3:13). According to Deuteronomy 28:15-68, a number of curses will come upon anyone who will not "obey the voice of the Lord." Well, the testimony of Scripture and the fact of experience is that, all of us have disobeyed the voice of the Lord and are consequently subject to the curse of the Law. New Covenant salvation enters at this point with the good news that Jesus Christ has (on our behalf) obeyed the voice of the Lord perfectly. Thus, if we would just trust what He has done for us in His atoning death, burial, and resurrection, then, His righteousness will become our righteousness, and the blessings of Abraham will come upon us in Christ Jesus.

Together, these realities make up the heart and soul of the New Covenant. Here we find our true identity as individuals, and as members of the corporate Body of Christ (the Church).

It will be helpful, at this point, to contrast the Covenant of the Old Order with the Covenant of the New Order. The writer of the Epistle to the Hebrews explain:

> But now hath he obtained a more excellent ministry, by how much also he is the mediator of a better covenant, which was established upon better promises.

The key word here is "better." The Covenant of the Old Order was good (whether it was the Adamic, Noahic, Abrahamic, Mosaic or the Davidic). But, the word is that the New Covenant is "better." Observe the following visual contrasts and see just how much better the New Covenant is than the Old Covenant:

Old Covenant	New Covenant
1.Came by sinful man	1. Came by the sinless Christ
2.Temporary	2. Permanent
3.Incomplete	3. Complete
4.Conditional	4. Unconditional
5.Written on stones	5.Written in the heart
6.External manifestation	6. Internal appropriation
7.Obedience demanded	7. Obedience enabled
8.Failed due to man's disobedience	8. Succeeds through the obedience of Christ
9.Man's heart was wrong	9. Man's heart is changed
10.Of the letter	10. Of the Spirit
11.Man says, "I ought."	11. Man says, "I can."
12.Provisional and preparatory	12.Ultimate and sufficient
13.Condemnation and death	13. Righteousness and life

14.Of passing glory	14. Of permanent glory
15.Provided covering	15. Providing cleansing
16.Closed by the death of Jesus	16. Initiated by the death, burial and resurrection of Jesus.
17.For Israel	17. For all who believe

THE TERMS OF THE NEW COVENANT

Every covenant has binding terms and the New Covenant is no different. The Lord Jesus Christ, first of all, requires of all who would abide in Him that we be quick to repent of our sins. This will involve a four-fold process: **Consideration** of our ways in light of the truth of God's Word; **sorrow** for transgressions; **renunciation** of old ways and a **change** of behavior. Also, under the New Covenant, we are required to "trust in" and "agree with" the Lord and His Words, in everything. This trust (or faith) is the channel through which the benefits of the Covenant are received (Mk. 1:15; Acts 20:21; Heb. 11:6). New Covenant believers are also required to lovingly obey the commandments of Jesus Christ, sometimes called, "The Law of Christ" (Jn. 14:15; I Cor. 9:20; I Jn. 3:22-24). Jesus Christ, Himself, is our example here. His entire life was aligned with the Word and commandments of the Father (Jn. 8:29). Moreover, in Matthew 5:17-19 Jesus made it clear that He was all about fulfilling the Law and the Prophets, and anyone who dared to break one of the least of the commandments would be called least in the kingdom order of God. Thus, the connection He makes in John 14:21 is consistent with His overall teachings. If we truly love Him, we will love and obey the Father's Word also.

Study the following partial list of commandments. Jesus gave them to us and keeping them is not optional (Jn. 3:36; 14:21, 23;

15:8-10, 13-14; Lk. 6:46-49; Jas. 1:22: II Pet. 1:5-11; I Jn. 2:3-6). A special measure of the Father's love, plus a special experience of the indwelling presence of the Father and the Son is promised to those believers who really love the Lord and keep His commandments. Such obedience is a practical expression of the New Creation life that was imparted as a gift of grace in regeneration. (Study Mt. 22:37-40; I Jn. 5:3; II Jn. 6; Rom. 13:8-10).

NEW TESTAMENT COMMANDS OF JESUS	
1.Love God (Mt. 22:37-38).	14. Fast unto God in secret (Mt. 6:16-18)
2.Love your neighbor (Mt. 22:39-40; Jn. 13:34).	15. Make the things of God top priority (Mt. 6:19-34).
3.Let your life be a witness (Mt. 5:13-16).	16. Be careful of being judgmental (Mt. 7:1-5)
4.Pursue righteousness (Mt. 5:17-20)	17.Reverence that which is holy (Mt. 7:6)
5.Seek reconciliation (Mt. 5:21-26)	18.Go to God with your requests (Mt. 7:8)
6.Maintain the sanctity of marriage (Mt. 5:27-32; 19:1-9)	19.Do to others what you want done to you (Mt. 7:12).
7.The making of oaths prohibited (Mt. 5:33-37)	20.Follow the strait and narrow path (Mt. 7:15-23)
8.Retaliation is forbidden (Mt. 5:38-42)	21.Judge character and ministry by their fruit (Mt. 7:15-23)
9.Love your enemies (Mt. 5:43-47)	22.Walk in obedience (Mt. 7:24-27).
10.Be perfect even as God is perfect (Mt. 5:48).	23.Take communion in remembrance of Jesus (Mt. 26:26-29).
11.Give alms in secret (Mt. 6:1-4)	24.Baptize in the Name of Jesus (Mt. 28:18-19)

12.Pray earnestly and simply in secret (Mt. 6:5-13)	25.Proclaim the Gospel with Holy Ghost power (Mk. 16:15-18)
13.Forgive that you may be forgiven (Mt. 6:14-15; 18:21-35).	26.Be filled with the Holy Spirit (Lk. 24:49)

A BOND IN BLOOD

The phrase translated "to make a covenant," in the Old Testament, literally means "to cut a covenant." In Genesis 15:7-21 we have an example of the ritual ceremony that's commonly associated with the establishment of this kind of bond. Abraham, in obedience to the Word of God, divides or cuts up a number of animals and lays the pieces over against one another. God then (symbolically represented by a "smoking fire pot and a flaming torch") passed between the cut up pieces of animals. The effect of all of this was the "making" or "cutting" of a covenant.

The dismembered animals represent the curse that the covenant maker calls down on himself if he should, for any reason, fail to keep his word. Some teachers have correctly referred to this as a "pledge to the death at the point of commitment."

I like the phrase, "bond in blood" or "bond of life and death." This is what a covenant really is. The writer of the Epistle to the Hebrews makes the point that, "without the shedding of blood there is no remission of sins" (Heb. 9:22). Blood is important here. According to Leviticus 17:11, "The life is in the blood"; hence, the shedding of blood, in the letter to the Hebrews, represents a judgment on life.

In his book entitled, *The Christ of the Covenants,* Dr. O. Palmer Robertson says,

"The Biblical imagery of the blood-sacrifice emphasizes the interrelation of life and blood. The pouring out of life-blood signifies the only way of relief from covenant obligations once incurred. A covenant is a bond-in-blood, committing the participants to loyalty on pain of death. Once the covenant relationship has been entered, nothing less than the shedding of blood may relieve the obligations incurred in the event of covenant violation."

It is in this context of covenantal death that the death of Jesus Christ must be understood. Christ died for us i.e., in our place. This truth will be studied in more detail later; but, suffice it to say now that, the precious blood of Jesus is what makes the New Covenant valid for believers. Because of covenantal violation, we were condemned to die. Christ took upon Himself the curses of the covenant (Dt. 28:15-68) and died in our place, thus opening up a new and living way into the presence and the provision of God. By the blood of Jesus Christ, a new and eternal bond is established between us and the Father. This is clearly taught in the following Scriptures:

¹¹ But when Christ appeared as high priest of the good things that have come, then through the greater and more perfect tent (not made with hands, that is, not of this creation) ¹² he entered once for all into the Holy Place, taking not the blood of goats and calves but his own blood, thus securing an eternal redemption.

Hebrews 9:11-12 RSV

The Apostle Paul said something in his Second Epistle to the Corinthians that is directly applicable to this lesson on the New Covenant. He says,

What this means is that those who become Christians become new persons. They are not the same anymore, for the old life is gone. A new life has begun.

II Corinthians 5:17 NLT

CONCLUSION

It is important to see here that, we are not now living our lives under the Old Covenant. Old things have passed away. We have a "New Deal" with God that's better than the old arrangement set up under Moses. It's a better covenant because it's based upon better promises. Moreover, the broad provisions of this better covenant pertains to life and godliness. In other words, whatever your need (whether it's natural or spiritual) God has made provision for meeting that need in the New Covenant.

The goal of God's covenantal dealings is the gathering and sanctifying of a people from every nation, tribe, people-group and language who will, at some point, inhabit the New Jerusalem in a renewed world order (Rev. 7:9; 21:1-2). The Apostle John describes the fullest expression of this covenant in this way: "They will be his people and God Himself will be with them and be their God" (Rev. 21:3). Toward this goal, God is now ordering the course of all things.

FOOD FOR THOUGHT AND DISCUSSION

God's covenant with Israel was **preparation** for the coming of God Himself in the person of Jesus Christ, to fulfill all of His promises and to give substance to the shadows cast by the Old Testament types (Isa. 40:10; Mal. 3:1; Jn. 1:14; Heb. 7-10). Jesus Christ, the Mediator of the New Covenant, offered Himself as the true and final sacrifice for sin. He obeyed the Law perfectly, and, as the second Adam, He (along with those united to Him by faith) inherited all of the covenant blessings of peace and fellowship with God in His renewed creation. The Old Testament arrangements were **temporary** and became obsolete when **they were realized in Christ.**

J.I. Packer goes on to say this:

The covenant framework embraces the entire economy of God's sovereign grace. Christ's heavenly ministry continues to be that of the "mediator of a new covenant" (Heb. 12:24). Salvation is covenant salvation: justification and adoption, regeneration and sanctification are covenant mercies, election was God's choice of future members of his covenant community, the church; baptism and the Lord's Supper, corresponding to circumcision and Passover, are covenant ordinances; God's law is covenant law, and keeping it is the truest expression of gratitude for covenant grace and of loyalty to our covenant God. Covenanting with God in response to his covenanting with us should be a regular devotional exercise for all believers, both in private and at the Lord's Table. An understanding of the covenant of grace guides us through and helps us to appreciate all the wonders of God's redeeming love.

In light of this, would it be wrong to conclude that, the church is in the New Covenant? For an excellent and quiet refreshing commentary on this issue, study the article below: **Is The New Covenant for Israel or the Church?** In my opinion, Sam Storms is, "hands down" the best kept secret in the land! See his book, **Kingdom Come,** chapter six, "Who Are The People of God? Israel, The Church, and Replacement Theology."

2

JESUS CHRIST: GOD AND MAN

Many years ago, our African forefathers expressed what they believed about Jesus Christ in special documents called, "creeds". The Apostles Creed is one of the oldest of such documents. The African creed called, "Amakniyou" is another. Together, these statements preserve an ancient picture of our Lord that is very real and very meaningful. It is a picture that is grounded in the revelation of Scripture, and it is something that we are commissioned to publish throughout the length and breadth of the nations of the world (Mk. 16:15-16; Acts 1:8). The following quotation is a powerful summary of the historic Christian faith with respect to our Lord, Jesus Christ:

> I believe in Jesus Christ His only Son, our Lord, who was conceived by the Holy Spirit, born of the Virgin Mary, suffered under Pontius Pilate, was crucified, died and buried: **He descended** into hell; the third day **He rose again** from the dead; **He ascended** into heaven, and **sitteth on the right hand of God** the Father Almighty; from thence **He shall come to judge** the living and the dead...

Along with the Nicene Creed, this statement is a part of the standard by which other confessions may be judged. They combine natural truth and supernatural truth (facts of sense experience and facts of faith) in a clear and concise declaration of the only Savior that we have.

An Afrocentric Overview

The Scriptures teach that, in the early part of the first century, a special baby was born to a young African girl whose name was, Mary. She named the baby, "Jesus," which means "God is Savior." He was distinguished from other young men by the title, "Christ" i.e., "Anointed One" or "Messiah." Many people simply referred to Him as Jesus, the Christ.

In the natural, Jesus was a Hamitic Jew. In other words, He was a member of the Black Hebrew-Israelite people who lived in classical or Northeast Africa (known in modern times as the Middle East). This racial group was a mixture of Chaldeans, Egyptians, Midianites, Ethiopians, Cushites, Babylonians and other dark skinned peoples. All of these groups were previously mixed with black people groups in Central Africa. [1]

Spiritually speaking, Jesus is "The Son of God". This designation signifies the unique and eternal relationship that he has with the One True God of the Patriarchs. He is the "only-one-of-a-kind" Son of God (John 1:14, 18; 6:16; 18). Actually, this title means that Jesus was "God manifested in the flesh." To be a real Christian, one must believe and confess that Jesus Christ is the Son of God (I Jn. 2:23).

Our ancestors also called Jesus, "Lord." This title points to the divine sovereignty, and in the New Testament, it is used in reference to both the Father and the Son (Mk. 12:29, 36; Lk. 4:8). By calling Jesus, "Lord," the earliest Christians confessed that the power, honor, and glory due to God the Father was also due to God the Son. This confession was based upon the clear revelation that, Jesus, the Son of God, actually existed in the form of God Himself. To these believers, Jesus was divine (Phil. 2:5-11).

The African creed, "Amakniyou," moreover teaches that, Jesus entered into this world by a supernatural act of power. Article five says it like this:

> "Who in the last days was pleased to become man, and took flesh from our Lady Mary, the holy Virgin, without seed of man, and grew like men without sin or evil; neither was guile found in his mouth."

Some people, at this point, stress what is called, "Immaculate Conception." However, our forefathers did not teach that Mary was without sin.[2] Their focus was upon two things: number one, she was not sexually active. Number two, she lived in the favor of God. Moreover, it was clear to them that Mary was a member of the fallen race of Adam and thus needed to be "born again" just like everyone else.

The real emphasis in the "Amakniyou" creed is placed upon Jesus and not Mary. He was conceived by God Himself, apart from any human father (Isa. 7:14; Mt. 1:18-25; Lk. 1:26-38). This means that Jesus did not inherit any "original sin." Also, because of the nature of his conception, His manhood was untainted, and His behavior, attitudes, motives and desires were faultless (Jn. 8:29; Heb. 4:15).

To be sure, the picture of the Lord that is set forth here poses a major challenge to the erroneous teachings of several religions. Such groups as Jehovah's Witnesses, The Church of Jesus Christ of Latter

Day Saints, The Nation of Islam, Orthodox Judaism and the Pan African Orthodox Christian Church (Shrine of the Black Madonna) advance a view of Jesus that is in total opposition to the truth of the Holy Scriptures. They preach what the apostle Paul calls "a different gospel." Such a "gospel" evokes the judgment of God. Observe the actual text:

> **8 Let God's curse fall on anyone, including myself, who preaches any other message, let him be forever cursed.**
>
> **9 I will say it again: If any one preaches any other gospel than the one you welcomed, let God's curse fall upon that person.**
>
> **Galatians 1:8-9**

Among other things, this passage reminds us of the importance of having the right message and the right Jesus. In another key passage the apostle stated the case very well:

> **1 Now let me remind you, dear brothers and sisters, of the Good News I preached to you before. You welcomed it then and still do now, for your faith is built on this wonderful message.**
>
> **2 And it is this Good News that saves you if you firmly believe it — unless, of course, you believed something that was never true in the first place.**
>
> **I Corinthians 15:1-2 NLT**

The Pre-existent Christ

The Scriptures also teach that Jesus actually existed before he was born. Indeed this is a radical statement; but, the Biblical support is tremendous.

1. Names given to Him in the Old Testament indicate this. Note Micah 5:2 and Habakkuk 1:12 where the phrase "from of old" teaches us that, what the Father is, the Son is also i.e., everlasting (Micah 5:2; Hab. 1:12; Isa. 9:6).

2. Jesus Himself claimed to be pre-existent. "I Am" is a reference to the sacred name of God, "YHWH' or Jehovah (Jn. 8:58; Ex. 3:14-15).

3. The work of creation (which is said to have been done by Christ) could only have been accomplished if He existed before His birth (Co. 1:16).

4. Jesus is called "The Word" in John 1:1 and as such, He is the eternal utterance or expression of the person and thought of God (Jn. 1:3-5, 9, 14-18; 14:9-11; Col. 2:9).

Such a Jesus as this will, understandably, not fit into carnal or worldly type thinking. But then again, any other Jesus would be totally unable to save us from the penalty and the power of sin.

The Offices of Christ

The Bible uses three terms to designate the offices of Christ. He is God's anointed Prophet, Priest and King. The Greek word "prophētēs" is the technical term for "one who speaks for God." It suggests the ideas of proclamation, preaching and teaching (informing). Foretelling the future was also involved but, not always. Basically, the prophet was a mouth for God to use. Sometimes, he was given the privilege of "seeing" God's message in his mind, via dreams or visions. Of course, whenever this happened, the prophet was more accurately called a seer.

Jesus fulfilled this ministry in the highest sense by proclaiming again and again that the promises of the Old Testament prophets (what they foresaw) were being fulfilled in His own life (Lk. 4:16-21). Oftentimes, He advised His disciples that the words He spoke actually came from the Father. Toward the end of His public ministry, Jesus had a lot to say about things that were yet to come (Mt. 24-25). The point in all of this is that, Jesus clearly fulfilled the ministry of a prophet of the One True God.

Jesus Christ also fulfilled the office of Priest. By definition, a priest is a consecrated person who represents God to the people, and the people to God. In the Old Testament, priests were from the tribe of Levi and offered both sacrifices and gifts to celebrate the Lord and to obtain God's favor and forgiveness.

Unlike the Levitical priests, Jesus was after the line of Melchizedek (Heb. 7:15-17). He actually became a priest in that order by the power of a life that could not be destroyed. He didn't need cleansing; neither did He need to offer a sacrifice for His own personal sin. Why? He was sinless. The sacrifice He offered was Himself. His own blood was shed as an atonement to cover the sins of the entire world. The writer of the Epistle to the Hebrews has this to say:

> **25 Therefore he is able, once and forever, to save everyone who comes to God through him. He lives forever to plead with God on their behalf.**

26 He is the kind of high priest we need because he is holy and blameless, unstained by sin. He has now been set apart from sinners, and he has been given the highest place of honor in heaven.

27 He does not need to offer sacrifices every day like the other high priests. They did this for their own sins first and then for the sins of the people. But Jesus did this once for all when he sacrificed himself on the cross.

28 Those who were high priests under the law of Moses were limited by human weakness. But after the law was given, God appointed his Son with an oath, and his Son has been made perfect forever.

Hebrews 7:25-28 NLT

Finally, Jesus fulfilled the office of King. He has broken the powers of death, hell and the grave, and is seated in the place of supreme authority at the right hand of God. Isaiah foresaw Him and His day (Isa. 9:6) and proclaimed it. John, the beloved apostle, wrote in the Book of Revelation about the Lamb of God reigning as King of kings (Rev. 5:6-13; 11:15). Presently, people of faith know that Jesus reigns as the Great Head of the Church in absolute, imperial authority (Eph. 1:22-23). Indeed, He is our Lord and King and it is His Rule in the midst of the Church that produces righteousness, peace and joy in the Holy Spirit (Rom. 14:17).

The Scriptures teach that Christ will continue in this Kingly session until all of His enemies (including death) are completely destroyed. Death, which is the last enemy, will cease to be at the consummation of the ages according to the teachings of Scripture.

Kenosis or "Self-Emptying"

The apostle Paul says something in his Epistle to the Philippians that has been difficult for many people to understand. The actual text says,

> **Who, being in the form of God, did not consider it robbery to be equal with God, but made Himself of no reputation, taking the form of a bond slave, and coming in the likeness of men.**
>
> **Philippians 2:6-7 NASB**

Some people, after reading this passage conclude that, in some way, Jesus emptied Himself of some or all aspects of His deity when He came to earth. Progressive Full-Gospel teachers have consistently believed that, you cannot subtract any divine attributes from Jesus without changing the character of His person. I personally think this is a major observation. Is there a correct view of the doctrine of kenosis? I think so.

A proper statement of the doctrine of the kenosis or self-emptying of Jesus should involve the following points. First of all, the emphasis in this doctrine must be placed upon the veiling of the pre-incarnate glory and excellence of Christ. He talked about this in John 17:5. Obviously this shared glory was not something that was being displayed at the time. It was veiled or covered up.

Secondly, this doctrine stresses the condescension of taking upon Himself "the likeness of sinful flesh" (Rom. 8:3). More than the subtraction of deity, "emptied Himself" is best understood to mean the addition of humanity with its subsequent limitations. [4]

Finally, a proper statement of this doctrine focuses attention upon the voluntary non-use of some of His divine attributes during the time of His earth-walk. It's important to see here that choosing not to use His divine attributes is not the same as saying that He gave them up (Mt. 24:36).

CONCLUSION

Two African fathers have greatly influenced what we believe about Jesus Christ. They are St. Athanasius, and St. Cyril of Alexandria. The following is a summary statement of what they taught:

Jesus Christ is **one person** who has **two natures:** a human nature and a divine nature. Both of these natures are complete in themselves. They are, moreover, **united but not mixed** or confounded so as to produce a third nature. Because of this union of two natures in one person, Jesus Christ is the perfect mediator between God and man; and He is also the only qualified liberator of the human race (I Tim. 2:5; 3:16; Col. 2:9).

In a nutshell, this is what we believe and confess, to the glory of God the Father.

FOOD FOR THOUGHT AND DISCUSSION

There are a number of legitimate ways of expressing the significance of Jesus Christ for the world and for the individual Christian. He is a friend, liberator, king, doctor, lawyer, judge, sacrificial lamb, rock, mother, teacher, example, messiah, mediator etc. All of these expressions are valid; however, they are not exhaustive. New models and metaphors will emerge as the gospel is taken to new "people-groups" and cultures. The question arises, "is there a basic, universal Christian belief about Jesus Christ that all of these diverse metaphors must build upon? Is there, in other words, a standard by which new models and metaphors can be judged?

Roger E. Olson says, yes there is. In his book, *The Mosaic of Christian Belief* (Downers Grove, Illinois, InterVarsity Press 2002), p. 241 he says, "It (the standard) is the one agreed upon by the leaders of the early, undivided church that was simply an outworking in formal language of the apostolic witness itself:

"Jesus Christ is God incarnate; one unified person — the eternal Son of God equal with the Father; of two distinct but never separate natures, both human and divine."

To be sure, this is a mystery. It says a lot and yet, it leaves a lot unsaid that particular cultures and situations need to know about. Basically, what it does is rule out those models of Christology that would reduce Jesus Christ to something other than who and what the Bible reveals.

What do you think about "The Jesus Creed"/ (See Appendix B)

3

UNLIMITED ATONEMENT

Every student of the life of Christ will readily acknowledge that there was a very strong sense of urgency and purpose that dominated the heart of Jesus as He moved in and out among the people. He was conscious of having a particular work or assignment to complete. This consciousness literally consumed Him. He talked about it all the time. Observe!

> **Jesus saith unto them, My meat is to do the will of him that sent me, and to finish his work.**
>
> **John 4:34**

> **But Jesus answered them, My Father worketh hitherto, and I work.**
>
> **John 5:17**

> **I have glorified thee on the earth; I have finished the work which thou gavest me to do.**
>
> **John 17:4**

Hence, when He [Christ] entered into the world, He said, Sacrifices and offerings You have not desired, but instead You have made ready a body for Me [to offer];

6 In burnt offerings and sin offerings You have taken no delight.

7 Then I said, Behold here I am, coming to do Your will, O God — [to fulfill] what is written of Me in the volume of the Book.

Hebrews 10:5-7 AMP

We know now that, the particular work that Jesus was sent to accomplish was the work of unlimited atonement. This was "the will of the Father" to which He was totally committed. And on the basis of the completion of this work, sinners from every "people group" in the world would be given the opportunity to come out of spiritual darkness and experience God's marvelous light" (I Pet. 2:9-10). Moreover, true believers in the Lord Jesus Christ (on the basis of this same finished work) could enjoy a rich inheritance of "spiritual blessings in heavenly places in Christ" (Eph. 1:3). [1] None of this was by accident.

A PLANNED EVENT

When the Apostles' Creed says that Jesus "suffered under Pontius Pilate, was crucified, died and was buried," we must see that His violent death on the cross was a part of God's eternal program of redemption. It was, in other words, a planned event. This is exactly what the Scriptures teach (Acts 2:3; 4:27-28; Ps. 2:1-2). The prophet Isaiah explains this same truth in his message about the death of the Righteous Servant of the Lord (Isa. 53:10-12 NLT). To be sure, by design Jesus came to suffer and to die; but then, what does that mean? Roger Olson raises a number of questions at this point that serious students of the Bible must address. While all Christians have always agreed that Jesus Christ is the Savior of the world, they have not always agreed on the details of *how* Christ saves humans. Was his very life as the incarnate one—his union of deity with humanity—somehow saving? If so, how is that to be understood and explained? Was his life as the God-man on earth perhaps only or primarily a journey to the crucifixion where, by his death, he accomplished salvation for humanity? If so, how is his death saving? Why did he (or anyone) have to die in order for humanity to be reconciled to God? Did Christ's saving work on behalf of humanity actually accomplish salvation? That is, was it an objectively "done deal"? Or is there something for humans to do? Is a certain response to Jesus Christ's life and death required for anyone to benefit from his work? These and other questions have been asked by inquiring minds over the centuries. They are fair and reasonable questions which Christian theologians have attempted to answer.

Our understanding of the true meaning of the sufferings of Jesus Christ centers around at least three words. The first word is "vicarious." This word means, "totally for the benefit of another." Thus, the sufferings and death of Jesus Christ were endured "for our sake" and "in our stead." In a very real sense, He was our substitute (Isa. 53:5-6; I Cor. 15:3; II Cor. 5:21; I Pet. 3:18).

This is a powerful revelation. Jesus did not die for His own sins because, he was sinless (Jn. 8:46; I Pet. 2:22). He had no personal sins. The prophet Isaiah said, "he was pierced for our transgression." The apostle Paul pointed out that, "Christ died for our sins according to the Scriptures." This is why Progressive Full-Gospel Christians speak so emphatically of the "substitutionary" work of Christ. They see this as something deeply embedded in the Scriptures.

The second word supporting our understanding of the sufferings of Jesus Christ is the word, "satisfaction" or "propitiation." This word means "to appease" or to render favorable." The idea here is that, one brings an offering, gift or sacrifice of sufficient value in order to satisfy the wrath of another. Hence, the sufferings of Jesus Christ on the cross were of sufficient value to satisfy or appease the holy wrath and judgment of God.

Finally, our understanding of the sufferings of Jesus Christ necessitates an understanding of the word, "atonement." The Hebrew word "kaphar" comes from an Akkadian word meaning "to wipe away." In theology, the basic sense of the word is "to expiate" or "to remove." This is more than simply "to cover." Thus, "atonement" refers to that act of God whereby our sins are removed or "expiated" by the blood of Jesus Christ (see Jn. 1:29; and Heb. 9:26). With sin out of the way, real fellowship [Grk. "koinonia"] is now a present possibility for all men. [3]

THE EXTENT OF THE ATONEMENT

Progressive teachers insist that, when they talk about the universality of grace, they do not mean universalism or ultimate reconciliation. The key point they make is that, God in His grace was genuinely at work in His Son Jesus Christ **providing the potential of salvation** for every human being everywhere. [4] This is just the opposite of what some reformed Christians teach. They contend that, divine grace, while it is unlimited in its sufficiency, is never the less quite limited when it comes to its efficiency. According to this tradition, grace does not universally and indiscriminately provide every human being with an opportunity for a redemptive relationship to God that includes the forgiveness of sin and the promise of eternal life. To the contrary, grace (as they explain it), in its effective outworking, is only for a select few, who have been chosen by God from eternity. Non-elect persons are outside the reach of God's effective grace.

The Bible teaches that, Christ died for the whole world. In some places this is called "unlimited atonement," which is to say that, Christ died for everyone, but His saving work is effected only in those who actually repent of their sins and believe the gospel. In His *Lectures in Systematic Theology,* H. C. Thiessen says,

> The atonement is unlimited in the sense that it is available for all; it is limited in that it is effective only for those who believe. It is available for all, but efficient only for the elect. [5]

(In this connection, see also Isa. 53:6; Mt. 11:28; Rom. 5:18; II Cor. 5:14-15; I Tim. 4:10; II Pet. 3:9).

A.H. Strong summarizes the sense in which Jesus Christ is said to be the Savior of the world in the following quotation:

> His death secured for all men a delay in the execution of the sentence against sin, space for repentance and the common blessings of life which have been forfeited by transgression; it removed from the mind of God every obstacle to the pardon of the penitent and restoration of the sinner, except his willful opposition to God and rejection of Him; it procured for the unbeliever the powerful incentives to repentance presented in the cross, by means of the preaching of God's servants and through the work of the Holy Spirit; it provided salvation for

those who die in infancy, and assured its application to them; and it makes possible the final restoration of creation itself. [6]

Thus, the Scriptures teach that the death of Jesus Christ targeted both "the elect" and "the world." There is no either/or situation here. The atonement is both universal and particular. By His death on the cross, the sin debt of all men everywhere has been paid. This being true, what should we be telling the world? The Biblical answer to this question is both clear and simple. We must preach the "Good News" that Jesus paid it all and that sins are now forgiven. We must declare that the way leading to the "God-kind of life" is now open to whosoever believeth. Moreover, we must not hesitate to teach that all of this became possible because of the exchange that took place at Calvary.

THE GREAT EXCHANGE

It is important to see here that, on the cross an exchange took place. This aspect of the atonement is set forth in the Biblical doctrine of imputation (Philemon 17-18).

The Greek word "logizomai" is translated by three English words in the New Testament: count, reckon, and impute. It means, "to put to one's account." Actually, the Bible speaks of three major imputations and it is necessary to our study that we rightly understand these transactions.

There is, first of all, **the Imputation of the *Sin of Adam* and the Consequences of His Sin to the Race.** According to the Scriptures, we all have sinned in Adam. This truth is understood best by studying the New Testament passage in Hebrews 7:9-10. Here the author is sharing some revelation truths about Jesus Christ, our high priest. His key point is that the priesthood of Jesus is of a higher order than that of Levi. He says that Melchizedek was a "priest of God Most High." Abraham, the ancestor of Levi, paid tithes to Melchizedek, thereby showing that Melchizedek was the "greater one." Levi is thus said to be "the lesser one" because of his location "in the loins of Abraham" *at the time* that the patriarch paid tithes to the priest of God. Jesus is said to be a high priest after the order of this one, Melchizedek and *not* Levi.

This teaching helps us to understand how "we all sinned in Adam." We were in his loins when he willfully disobeyed the Word of God.

Secondly, there is the **Imputation of the Sin of the Race to Jesus Christ on the Cross.** Study these key Bible verses: II Corinthians 5:21; I Peter 2:24; Matthew 8:17; Isaiah 53:4ff. Observe, in this connection, the usage of the terms, "made to be sin" (actually Jesus was made to be the offering for sin), "laid on Him," "took our infirmities," "bore our sicknesses" and "bare our sins." It is important to note here that both sin and sickness are dealt with in the atonement. Also, (and this is very key) Jesus did *not* bear our sins in His *spirit.* Nowhere does the Bible ever say that our sins were borne anywhere other than in the *flesh.* According to I Peter 3:18, Jesus was only "put to death in the body," not his spirit!

Finally, there is the **Imputation of the "Righteousness of God" to the Believer.** Study again II Corinthians 5:21 plus I Corinthians 1:30 and Philippians 3:7-9. The plain teaching of these Scriptures is that, the only righteousness that God accepts is His own (Isaiah 54:17; 64:6). Therefore, if we are to be accepted by God, then, we must come to adorn that righteousness which is only "from above." Once this transaction is complete i.e., the transference of **our** sin to Christ and **His** righteousness to us, then, in keeping with the rule given in Deuteronomy 25:1, God the Father can "legally" declare that we are justified.

Derek Prince gives a more concise picture of the exchange that took place at the cross. He says,

> "At the cross, Jesus the Son of God took upon Himself all the evil due by justice to the sons of Adam, so that in return the sons of Adam might receive all the good due by eternal right to Jesus, the Son of God." [7]

Thus, the work of Jesus Christ on the cross changed Satan's position: he was "cast out" (Jn. 12:31) and he was "stripped of his weapons (Col. 2:15). Now, all members of the Adamic race may receive righteousness as a gift, and enter into fellowship and favor with God. Roger Olson summarizes his study of this subject as follows:

> What then is the Christian consensus about the atoning work of Christ? Is there any universal agreement of belief about Christ's saving achievement on humanity's behalf that defines authentic Christianity? In spite of tremendous diversity of language, imagery, theoretical explanations, theological constructs and even denominational distinctives about the subject, the unified voice of Christianity about this subject is clear: *Jesus Christ provides salvation for the world (humanity) by his life, death and resurrection.* I might add that this consensus includes belief that *God acted in Christ on the cross to reconcile the world (humanity) with himself and to make possible the forgiveness and transformation of sinners.* These exact words are not found in any creed or confessional statement, but they summarize well the belief of all Christians across two thousand years of church history. Anyone who denies them (as opposed to interprets them in a certain way) is in danger

of forfeiting his or her right to be considered an authentic Christian. Christianity is the saving work of Christ in his life, death and resurrection.

CONCLUSION

In conclusion, notwithstanding everything we've said about the extent of the atoning death of our Lord, "If He be not risen, then is our preaching vain, and your faith is also vain." The Apostle Paul goes on to say:

17 And if Christ has not been raised, then your faith is useless, and you are still under condemnation for your sins.

18 In that case, all who have died believing in Christ have perished!

19 And if we have hope in Christ only for this life, we are the most miserable people in the world.

I Corinthians 15:17-19 NLT

The faith of Progressive Full-Gospel Christians rests upon sound Biblical evidence that Jesus Christ our Lord and Savior arose bodily from among the dead. Observe!

1. Jesus made appearances that proved that He was not a ghost (Lk. 24:36-43).

2. His physical body was recognizable (Jn. 20:14-14-15; 20:26; 21:4, 12).

3. He appeared unto many eye witnesses.

   a. Mary Magdalene (Mk. 16:9-11)

b. Other women (Mt. 28:8-10)

c. Peter (Lk. 24:34; I Cor. 15:5)

d. The Emmaus disciples (Lk. 24:13-31)

e. The ten (Lk. 24:36; Jn. 20:19)

f. To 500 brethren (I Cor. 15:6)

g. The Ascension witnesses (Acts 1:6-11)

h. Paul (1 Cor. 15:8)

Among other things, this means that the work that Christ accomplished through His death on the cross has been accepted (Rom. 4:25; Phil. 2:5-11). Consequently, there is now available to every believer a vast inheritance of benefits that cover all things pertaining to life and godliness. These benefits are appropriated the same way you received eternal life: by faith!

FOOD FOR THOUGHT AND DISCUSSION

The Scriptures provide us with overwhelming testimony to the universality of the saving grace of God. Here is a selected number of passages that reveal the fact that God's purpose in Jesus Christ embraces the whole of the human race:

29 The next day John seeth Jesus coming unto him, and saith, Behold the Lamb of God, which taketh away the sin of the world.

John 1:29

16 For God so loved the world, that he gave his only begotten Son, that whosoever believeth in him should not perish, but have everlasting life.

John 3:16

17 For if by one man's offense death reigned by one' much more they which receive abundance of grace and of the gift of righteousness shall reign in life by one, Jesus Christ.

18 Therefore as by the offence of one judgment came upon all men to condemnation; even so by the righteousness of one the free gift came upon all men unto justification of life.

19 For as by one man's disobedience many were made sinners, so by the obedience of one shall many be made righteous.

20 Moreover the law entered, that the offence might abound. But where sin abounded, grace did much more abound:

21 That as sin hath reigned unto death, even so might grace reign through righteousness unto eternal life by Jesus Christ our Lord.

Rom. 5:17-21

32 For God hath concluded them all in unbelief, that he might have mercy upon all.

Rom. 11:32

6 Who gave himself a ransom for all, to be testified in due time.

I Tim. 2:6

9 But we see Jesus, who was made a little lower than the angels for the suffering of death, crowned with glory and honour; that he by the grace of God should taste death for every man.

Heb. 2:9

9 The Lord is not slack concerning his promise, as some men count slackness' but is longsuffering to us-ward, not willing that any should perish, but that all should come to repentance.

2 Peter 3:9

2 And he is the propitiation for our sins: and not for ours only, but also for the sins of the whole world.

I John 2:2

The explicit revelation of the universality of the atonement in the Scriptures cannot be denied. Study carefully Karl Rahner's statement below:

If we wish to be Christians, we must profess belief in the universal and serious salvific purpose of God towards all men. We know, to be sure, that this proposition of faith does not say anything certain about the individual salvation of man understood as something which has in fact already been reached. But God desires the salvation of everyone. And this salvation by supernatural grace is really intended for all those who lived before Christ—and also for those who have lived after Christ—in nations, cultures and epochs of a very wide range which were and are still completely shut off from the viewpoint of those living in the light of the New Testament.

The point here is that, God is truly at work in His Son Jesus Christ (and by His Holy Spirit) **providing the potential of salvation** for every human being. For this salvation to become actual, a person must respond in terms of faith. This is a mystery that must be preached with great grace and passion.

4

THE BENEFITS OF
THE ATONEMENT

In His death on the cross, Jesus purchased for us a vast inheritance that pertains to both life and godliness (II Pet. 1:3). Unfortunately, too few of us are even aware of the fact that there is such an inheritance. But, it's true anyhow. Because of Jesus Christ, we are rich — spiritually, materially and physically. The Apostle Paul says it like this:

For all things are yours;

²² Whether Paul, or Apollos, or Cephas, or the world, or life, or death, or things present, or things to come; all are yours;

²³ And ye are Christ's; and Christ is God's.

I Corinthians 3:31B-23

This is an amazingly comprehensive truth. It staggers our imagination and challenges our faith. Think about it! God has actually given us (His true people) all things. In other words, we are heirs of God and joint heirs with Jesus Christ (Rom. 8:16; Gal. 4:5-7). The world, life, death, things in the present, as well as things in the future: everything belongs to us! This is big! But now, do we dare act on this revelation? Is this for real? Are we to take this seriously or do we just explain it away and look in another direction?

The popular belief among professing Christians is that, God indeed has some really good things or benefits[1] laid up for the saints; but, they're not available now — in this life. The true benefits of our redemption (they say) will only be received in the life to come.

The Scriptures, on the other hand, clearly teach that, New Covenant salvation consists of realities, benefits and privileges that belong to us right now. The prophet Isaiah, for instance, mentions four key benefits of the atonement in chapter 53 of his book. They are as follows:

1. Forgiveness of Transgressions

2. Deliverance from Inbred Iniquities [2]

3. Peace

4. Physical Healing

These benefits belong to us now. They are never postponed until the next life. Jesus called them "the children's bread" in Matthew 15:26 and that's how we should view them. They are God-given realities that characterize our present life together in the New Creation of God.

LEGAL AND VITAL ISSUES

In order to further understand and appreciate these benefits, it is necessary that we spend some time looking at the legal and vital sides of New Covenant redemption. Some teachers prefer to use the terms "positional" and experiential." Regardless of the preference, the meaning of the terms are pretty clear. Both "legal" and "positional" refer to what God has done for us in His Son, the Lord Jesus Christ. These positional realities determine who we are, what we have and what we can do.

In this connection, John MacArthur makes the point that, the ignorance of many Christians is tragic. He observed that many believers stumble throughout their lives mainly because they don't know their covenant benefits. [3] Through the Prophet Hosea the Lord says, "My people are destroyed for lack of knowledge" (Hosea 4:6). In other words, they are cut off from God's blessing because of their ignorance. This ignorance has cost them dearly. In the same book referred to above, John MacArthur goes on to say:

> The Christian life is the experience of becoming in practice (or experience) what we already are in position. For every positional truth in the New Testament, there is a corresponding practice that we are to follow. [4]

It is important here that every believer understand that, because of what God has done *for* us, and because of what He has wrought *in* us and *to* us (positional realities), there is now inside of us a new code of conduct, and a new ethical dynamic. We have a new position and this demands a new lifestyle! Through the atonement, God has changed everything. What He has done is foundational. It is what supports the God-kind of life that Jesus talked about in John 10:10. This is why Satan fights so hard to keep us ignorant of legal or positional truth.

Study the chart at the end of this chapter, "Practicing Your Position" [5] and create, in your own words, an affirmation of faith for each positional truth in the left hand column.

I want to reemphasize the point that, these positional truths are foundational. All spiritual life and growth is grounded in them. Thus, our position is the source from which we derive certain basic characteristics.

Miles J. Stanford, in his discussion of "The Principle of Position" makes a very timely observation:

> When we are born again, the risen Lord Jesus is the source of our Christian life; in Him we are positioned before the Father, in whom we live, and move, and have our being (Acts 17:28). Our Father, in redeeming and recreating us, "raised us up together with Him, and seated us with Him in the heavenly places in Christ Jesus" (Eph. 2:6).[6]

This is very key. The believer who comes to really see his or her position in Christ will begin to experience the great benefits of the atonement as never before. His or her daily state is thus developed from the source of their eternal standing or position. That's what the left hand side of the "Practicing Your Position" chart is all about.

CONCLUSION

In concluding this section, meditate on the following Scripture and list every good thing which is in you in Christ Jesus. Write them down on 5x7 cards.

**That the communication of thy faith may become effectual
by the acknowledging of every good thing which is in you
in Christ Jesus.**

Philemon 6

The lesson here is that, our faith life will become more effective
as we acknowledge the legal or positional realities that pertain to us
in Christ. Acknowledging here means confessing or affirming "the
good things that are in us in Christ Jesus." This lines up with Romans
10:10.

Observe that, these "good things" that are within us are not our
own accomplishments. They are positional benefits i.e., things that
God has done for us based upon the blood of Jesus.

Satan's evil plan is to cause the people of God to focus their attention upon their past transgressions, failures, weaknesses and mistakes.
We must resist this demonic ploy by intentionally acknowledging the
great benefits of the atonement and not our sins. This sets our faith
on fire. Acting like we are who God says we are, acting like we have
what God says we have, and acting like we can do what God says
we can do will completely revolutionize the way we get along in the
world! Wow! What a difference the Lord makes!

FOOD FOR THOUGHT AND DISCUSSION

In the chart, "**Practicing Your Position**" no less than 28 "positional truths" are listed. These are "realities" that were applied to
us the instant we were "saved." I have personalized these truths as
follows:

1. I have "zoe" [the God-kind of life] in my spirit. I am spiritually alive and alert.

2. Sin no longer has dominion over me. I am "dead to sin and alive unto God."

3. I have been forgiven of **all** of my transgressions.

4. I have been made righteous and now "stand before God" just as if I had never sinned.

5. I am a legitimate child [off-spring] of God.

6. I am God's property.

7. I am an heir of God, and a joint heir of Jesus Christ.

8. I am blessed (right now) with all "**spiritual blessing**" in heavenly places.

9. In my spirit (my inner being) I am not of this world i.e., this perverse generation.

10. I am a true **servant-son** of God.

11. I am a **new creation** in Christ Jesus.

12. I am free from the law of sin and death.

13. I have been crucified to the world.

14. I am a source of light to the world.

15. I am victorious over all that is satanic and demonic.

16. I am holy and without blame.

17. I am free.

18. I am in Christ.

19. I am secure in Christ Jesus.

20. I have **peace with God**, and I possess **the peace of God** in my heart.

21. I am one with Jesus Christ and with my covenant brothers and sisters.

22. I stand in God's grace.

23. I abide in fellowship with the Lord and his people.

24. I reside in the joy of the Lord.

25. I am filled with and led by the Holy Spirit of God.

26. I am gifted by the Holy Spirit of God.

27. I am supernaturally empowered to do the business of the Father.

28. My faith works because I walk in divine love.

What do you think would happen in our local churches if every member would affirm these realities out loud everyday for the next 365 days?

PRACTICING YOUR POSITION

In Christ we are perfect positionally; but in practice we fall short. The Christian life is the experience of becoming in practice what we are in position. These positional truths are foundational. All spiritual life and growth is grounded in them. We can now live by a new code of conduct because of what God has done for us in Christ.

POSITION	PRACTICE
II Pet. 1:3-4	II Pet. 15-8
Eph. 1:3	Eph. 4:1
Col. 2:10	II Tim. 3:17
Heb. 10:14	Col. 4:12
	Heb. 13:20-21
We Are Spiritually Alive	**Live the Life**
Eph. 2:1, 4-5	Phil. 1:21
I Jn. 4:9	Gal. 2:20
Jn. 11:25; 14:19	Rom. 6:11-13
Acts 17:28	Titus 2:12
We are Dead to Sin	**Don't Give In to Sin**
Eph. 1:7	Rom. 6:11-15
I Jn. 1:9; 2:12	Col. 3:3
Col. 1:14	
We have been Forgiven	**Count On It!**
Eph. 1:7	Rom. 8:1, 33-34
I Jn. 1:9; 2:12	
Col. 1:14	

We have been Made Righteous Rom. 1:17; 3:21-26 Rom. 4:1, 3, 6; 5:17	**Live Righteously** II Tim. 2:22 I Jn. 3:7
We are Now the Children of God Eph. 1:4 II Tim. 2:19	**Act Like God's Children** Eph. 5:1 I Pet. 1:13-14
We are God's Possession Eph. 1:4 II Tim. 2:19	**Yield to God** Rom. 12:1 II Tim. 2:19-21
We are Blessed with All Spiritual Blessing in the Heavenlies Eph. 1:3; 2:6-7 I Pet. 1:3-4	**Cherish those Blessings** Col. 3:1-2
We have Heavenly Citizenship (Not of this world) Phil. 3:20 Jn. 17:14-16 I Jn. 5:4-5	**Live as Citizens of Heaven** I John 2:15 Col. 3:12 Jas. 1:27
We are Servants of God I Cor. 7:22-23 Rom. 6:22	**Act Like a Servant** Rom. 6:17-19; 12:11
We have New Life II Cor. 5:17	**Walk in New Life** Rom. 6:4
We are Free from the Law	**Yet Keep Fulfilling the Law** Gal. 5:1 Rom. 8:4

We have been Crucified to the World	Avoid Worldly Things
Gal. 1:4 Gal. 6:14-15	I John 2:15-17 Jas. 4:4 Rom. 12
We are Victorious Over Satan	Claim Victory
Rev. 12:9-11	II Cor. 7:1 Phil. 4:8
We are Holy and Without Blame	Live Holy Lives
Eph. 1:3, 10; 2:6, 13	I Jn. 3:7 I Peter 1:15-16 II Peter 3:14
We are Free	Enjoy Your Freedom
John 8:32	Gal. 5:1
We are In Christ	I Abide in Him
Eph. 1:3, 10; 2:6,13	**I Jn. 2:28**

We are secure in Christ	Enjoy Your Security
I Pet. 1:5 Rom. 8 Jn. 10:27-28	II Pet. 1:10
We are Possessors of Peace	Let it Rule
Rom. 5:1; 14:17 Jn. 14:27 Acts 10:38	Rom. 14:19 Col. 3:15

We are One Eph. 4:4-6; 1:9-10 I Cor. 12:13	**Life that Oneness** Eph. 4:3 Jn. 17:21
We are In Grace Rom. 6:1	**Live that Oneness** Eph. 4:3 Jn. 17:21
We Abide in Fellowship I Jn. 1:3-7	**Experience that Fellowship** I Cor. 10:20 Eph. 5:11
We are Joyful Rom. 5:2	**Experience that Joy** I Jn. 1:4 Jn. 15:11; 16:24
We are Spirit Indwelt and Led I Cor. 6:19-20 Rom. 12:5-6	**Yield to the Spirit's Control** Eph. 5 :18; 4:30 I Thes. 5:19 Gal. 5:25
We are Empowered for Service Acts 1:8 Eph. 3:20 II Cor. 4:7 II Tim. 1:7	**Claim and Demonstrate that Power** I Cor. 2:4 Phil. 3:10 Eph. 6:10 Phil. 4:13
We Walk in Love Rom. 5:5 I Jn. 2:5; 5:1	**Love!** I Pet. 1:22; 4:8 Jn. 13:34 I Jn. 3:18

5

THE PRESENT DAY MINISTRY OF JESUS CHRIST

The Church, for the most part, has not really majored in what is known as the "Session of Christ"[1] or "The Present Day Ministry in Heaven." This neglect has been costly to say the least. Untold thousands of believers have been resigned to a life void of victory just because they never learned about the kingly and priestly ministry of Christ at the right hand of the Father (Col. 3:1-2). It is important therefore that we see that the ministry and destiny of all the saints depends upon the work that our Lord is engaged in right now in the heavenlies. That work is preceded by two important events, the first of which is the resurrection of Christ. The second is the ascension of Christ into the heavens.

BIBLICAL PROOF OF THE ASCENSION

The Scriptural evidence supporting the belief that Jesus actually ascended and arrived in heaven is 3-fold:

1. Acts 1:9-11 teaches us that Jesus literally went to heaven just as He literally came to earth when He was conceived and born. He will also literally return again after the Great Tribulation (Mt. 24:29 ff).

2. Acts 2:33-36 teaches that, when Christ arrived in heaven, He received from the Father the promise of the Holy Spirit. Therefore, the Pentecostal outpouring is a proof of the ascension of our Lord.

3. Acts 7:55-56 tells us that Stephen (the first martyr in the Jerusalem Church) actually saw Jesus standing at the right hand of God, in heaven.

Thus, these selected references provide us with some very strong reasons as to why we do not question the credibility of the ascension of Jesus Christ. We believe that the ascension of our Lord was gradual, visible, bodily and associated with clouds. We moreover believe that His second coming will be marked by these same characteristics.

The Value of the Ascension of Christ

One of the first things we learn is that the ascension marked the end of the self-imposed limitations of Jesus (Phil. 2:5-8). Prior to this event, Jesus existed in "the form of God." This meant that He was the same in nature and essence as God. The difference was that, He did not think of this as something to be exploited for His own advantage. Therefore, he emptied Himself i.e., He took on the limitations of humanity. This involved a veiling of His pre-incarnate glory and the voluntary nonuse of some of His powers while on earth. The ascension ended this limitation. Also, the ascension marked the end of His sacrificial work on the cross. It is important to note that, the ascension did not mark the end of "signs and wonders." (The Book of Acts shows that the supernatural ministry of signs and wonders continues to this day).

According to the "high priestly prayer" that Jesus prayed in John 17:5, the ascension restored Him to His pre-incarnate glory in heaven. This is no small point. Because Jesus was exalted as the "God-man," the value of human life "in Christ" is beyond measure. [2] Finally, the ascension of our Lord provides a key connection between His earthly work and His heavenly work at the right hand of the Father. Actually, the heavenly work presupposes the earthly work. You can't have one without the other.

THE PRESENT POSITION OF CHRIST

The Scriptures reveal that the present position of Christ in heaven is one of universal Lordship and Authority. According to Acts 2:33-36, the Father has given "all power" to Christ and that power is now being used to "hold all things together."

> **For by him were all things created, that are in heaven, and that are in earth, visible and invisible, whether they be thrones, or dominions, or principalities, or powers: all things were created by him, and for him: [17] And He is before all things, and by him all things consist.**
>
> **Colossians 1:16-17**

Christ is moreover revealed as "seated" or enthroned far above all intelligences in absolute, complete authority. The Scriptures make it very clear that the goal or aim of this "seating" is to bring an end to all demonic rule, authority, power and opposition—even death (Eph. 1:20-21; I Cor. 15:24-28).

Christ is also identified as the Head of the Redeemed Community—the Church (Eph. 1:22-23). This is His present day governmental position. Note! Biblical headship has to do with authority, order, loving care, discipline, covering, protection, provision, responsibility and safety. As far as the Church is concerned, the risen and exalted Lord, Jesus Christ, is the one who supplies this headship, and all Ascension gift ministries (Apostles, Prophets, Evangelists, Pastors, and teachers), Elders and deacons must submit to Him in everything. Why? Because, He alone directs the Church, which is His Body.

The Lord Jesus Christ is moreover positioned as the bestower of gifts. In the New Testament, a gift is a God-given enablement that's wrought in and through the believer by the indwelling Holy Spirit. Stated differently, a gift is the Holy Spirit working in us to fulfill a certain divine purpose. A gift is therefore in no sense a human activity or skill that has been anointed or blessed by God. It is totally a divine undertaking.

It is also important to see here that there are different "kinds" of gifts referred to in the Scriptures. There is first of all the Ascension Gifts. In Ephesians 4:11-12 these five-fold ministries are given to the Church for a specific time and purpose:

Wherefore he saith, When he ascended up on high, he led captivity captive, and gave gifts unto men.

[11] And he gave some, apostles; and some, prophets' and some, evangelists; and some, pastors and teachers;

[12] For the perfecting of the saints for the work of the ministry, for the edifying of the body of Christ:

[13] **Till we all come in the unity of the faith, and of the knowledge of the Son of God, unto a perfect man, unto the measure of the stature of the fulness of Christ.**

Ephesians 4:8, 11-13

It is important to see here the involvement of the Father, the Son and the Holy Spirit in this aspect of building and operating the Church of God. Note! The Father gave His Son to be the Head of the church and the Savior of the world. The Son in turn gave Himself, the Holy Spirit and the five-fold ministry gifts mentioned above. These gifted men and women are actually extensions of the ministry of Christ flowing in and through the Church. Thus, all self-centeredness is eliminated.

Finally, the Holy Spirit is God's gift through Christ to the individual believer and the Church. The gifts referred to in I Corinthian 12:4, 7 (The Congregational Gifts) come from the Holy Spirit. Study the diagram below for further clarification.

THE FATHER GIVES THE SON.
John 3:16

THE SON GIVES GIFTED MEN AND WOMEN
Acts 5:32; Ephesians 4:8-16; 5:25
Apostles Prophets Evangelist Pastors Teachers
"For the perfecting of the saints, for the work of the ministry"

THE MANIFESTATION OF THE HOLY SPIRIT IS GIVEN TO EACH BELIEVER
I Corinthians 12:1-11

Gifts of Inspiration	Gifts of Demonstration	Gifts of Revelation
Prophecy	Faith	Word of Wisdom
Tongues	Miracles	Word of Knowledge
Interpretation	Healings	Discerning of Spirits

CONGREGATIONAL GIFTS [3]

The second "kind" of gift that is bestowed upon believers is said to be Congregational. See Romans 12:3-8 and I Corinthians 12:4-11. These are manifestations of the Spirit of God. They are various avenues of service in the Redeemed Community i.e., The Body of Christ.

Every Christian has a responsibility to find their grace-gift and minister therein. Study the following list [3] of giftings and functions for further insight.

1. Apostles — One sent as a messenger, the bearer of a commission, Church planter, spiritual father of Churches (Eph. 4:11; I Cor. 12:28).

2. Prophets — A spokesman for another, an interpreter for God, a seer, a divinely commissioned and inspired person, a foreteller of the future, gifted for the exposition of the truth (Acts 15).

3. Evangelists — One who announces glad tidings, one who enlarges and extends the kingdom of God, one who shares in edifying and building the Church (Eph. 4:11; Acts 21:8; II Tim. 4:5).

4. Pastors — one who tends the sheep, a shepherd, one who cares for the sheep. One who leads, feeds, waters and guards the sheep, guardian (Jn. 10:16; 21:16; I Pet. 5:2, 3)

5. Teachers — One who instructs, the occupation of teaching, someone qualified to instruct others, someone who imparts Bible truth to others (I Tim. 3:2; II Tim. 2:4; I Cor. 12:28; Rom. 12:6).

6. Elder — a senior man, seasoned in years and spiritual growth, presbyter of the Church (Acts 11:30; 14:23; 20:17; I Tim. 4:14; 5:17-19.

7. Preacher — herald, public messenger, proclaimer, publisher (as evangelist) (I Tim. 2:7; II Pet. 2:5).

8. Deacons — One who renders service ministry, the act of rendering relief and aid to another (Acts 6:1; 11:29; II Cor. 8:4.

9. Ministry — he who ministers, service ministry, the act of rendering relief and aid to another (Acts 6:1; 11:29; II Cor. 8:4).

10. Word of Wisdom — The quality of being wise by the Holy Spirit, a flash revelation given by the Spirit (I Cor. 12:8).

11. Word of Knowledge — The fact or state of knowing by the Holy Spirit. A revelation of facts not known by natural understanding as given by the Spirit (I Cor. 12:8).

12. Discerning of Spirits — To recognize clearly when the Spirit of God, spirit of error or the human spirit at work. Perception of error or truth (I Cor. 12:10).

13. Gifts of Faith — Special and supernatural faith given by the Spirit for the miraculous (I Cor. 12:9).

14. Gifts of Healing — Those who have various gifts or a gift of healing by the Spirit, restoring health (Acts 4:22, 30; I Cor. 12:9, 28, 30; Heb. 12:13).

15. Worker of Miracles — Works of power, those who do or perform miracles (I Cor. 12:28; I Thes. 1:5; I Cor. 4:19, 20; 2:4; II Tim. 1:7; Rom. 1:16).

16. Prophecy — He who prophesies, a gifted faculty of setting forth inspired utterance in a known language (Rom. 12:6; I Cor. 12:10; 13:2; I Tim. 1:18).

17. Diversities of Tongues — A speaker in kinds of tongues, those who speak languages they have never learned, by the Spirit (I Cor. 14:5, 13, 27; 12:30).

18. Interpreter of Tongues — Greek, "diermeanutees" = To interpret tongues or languages by the power of the Spirit (I Cor. 14:5, 13, 27; 12:30).

19. Helps — Those who help others, helpers, one who aids, assists, helps or supports the weak, do others service (I Cor. 12:28; Lk. 1:54; Acts 20:35; I Tim. 6:2).

20. Directors — Governments, pilotage, to control the course of a ship, to steer or direct the Church (Acts 27:11; Rev. 18:17; I Cor. 12:28).

21. Exhorter — To warn, to admonish, to be cheered or comforted, to entreat, to urge, persuasion or excitement (I Thes. 5:14; Tit. 1:9; I Cor. 14:3; Heb. 3:13; 10:25; II Cor. 1:4, 6; Acts 20:12).

22. He That Giveth — He that imparts, to share, to bestow, a distributor of alms, to give a part of what we have (Lk. 3:11; Rom. 1:11, 12:8; I Thes. 2;8; Eph. 4:28).

23. He That Ruleth — He that takes the lead, to set before, appoint with authority, to preside, govern, superintend (I Thes. 5:12; I Tim. 3:4, 5, 12; 5:17; Tit. 3:8, 14; Rom. 16:2).

24. He That Sheweth Mercy — Have compassion, to show gracious favor, saving mercy towards (I Tim. 1:13, 16; Rom. 9:15, 16, 18; Jude 23; Mt. 5:7; 6:2-4; 9:27; 15:22; Heb. 2:17).

25. Hospitality — To entertain or receive a stranger into one's home as an honored guest, to provide guests with food, shelter and protection (Rom. 12:6-8; Jude 23; Mt. 5:7; 6:2-4; 9:27; 15:22; Heb. 2:17).

26. Intercession — Intercessory Prayer (Heb. 7:25).

27. [Ministry of Music] — Singers, the choir, musicians, the Tabernacle of David (I Chr. 15:25)

28. Ministry of Comfort — (Jn. 14:26; 15:26).

29. Ministry of Counseling — (Isa. 9:6-9)

30. Personal Evangelism — (Jn. 4; Acts 8).

31. Mothers In Israel — (Judges 5).

32. Fathers in The Lord — (I Cor. 4:19-20).

The Lord Jesus is moreover positioned now as our High Priest who ever lives to make intercession for His own. Observe the following key points: This ministry is for saved persons only. It will go on in heaven as long as the saints are in the world (Jn. 17:19). Moreover, this intercessory work has to do with the weakness, the helplessness and the maturity of the saints. God knows our limitations and the strategy of the enemy. He is also pledged to take care of us through every trial (Lk. 22:31-32; Heb. 7:25).

Finally, Christ is our advocate, and as such, He pleads or argues our cause before the Father. He's like a lawyer. The Lord Jesus Christ now appears in heaven for us whenever we commit sins (Heb. 9:24;

I Jn. 2:1). Note! In our eyesight, our sins may not seem to be all that big. But, in the eyes of a Holy God, our sins are an open scandal in heaven (Ps. 90:7-8 NLT).

Thank God that Jesus Christ, our advocate, pleads our case on the basis of His own righteousness and His own shed blood. He does this right in the face of the accuser of the brethren (Rev. 12:10). In this way, He establishes our eternal security (Rom. 8:34).

CONCLUSION

So, what is Christ doing now? Is He involved in any way with the affairs of the Church? Well, hopefully we've pointed out some clear, Biblical answers that will settle the issue. The New Testament reveals the heavenly activity of Jesus as follows:

1. He is standing ready to act (Acts 7:56; Rev. 1:1-16; 14:1).

2. He is walking among the saints (Rev. 2:1).

3. He is riding to battle (Rev. 19:11-16).

4. He is ruling at the right hand of the Father (Heb. 1:3).

At the same time, we read that Christ indwells His Church and imparts to it His own eternal life. Even the "Body ministry" that is so characteristic of Church life is, in all actuality, Christ living His life through His corporate people. Both the ascension gifts and the congregational gifts of the Spirit are means by and through which the heavenly session of our Lord makes its impact upon the earth. All in all, through the present-day ministry of Jesus Christ, God is calling out a people. He is forming a community. He is building His Church. He is moreover empowering and sanctifying this called out people to be His authorized visible representative in all the earth until He comes again.

THE GOSPEL OF
THE KINGDOM

The Bible tells us that in the midst of an end-time" situation of unrest and upheaval, a message from God will be proclaimed in all the world about a kingdom (government) that is unshakeable, unmovable and established (Mt. 24:14). This message will contain the inspired account of how God has dealt with the sin problem and its consequences. It will be preached by holy men and women of God who will be supernaturally "moved or carried along by the Holy Spirit" (II Pet. 1:21).

Jesus said that the preaching of this Gospel would actually be a witness to the nations, a sign of the end of the age and of the second coming.

A WORKING DEFINITION

Obviously, it is not enough just to say that the Gospel means "good news." To be sure, it is "good news"; however, the NT sense of the word cannot be determined from its secular usage alone. The earliest apostles were Greek speaking Jews who were steeped in the

OT Scriptures and culture. For them, the background for the NT usage of the word Gospel ("euangelion") was found in such passages as Isaiah 40:9; 41:27; 52:7; 61:1 and their contexts.

In this OT context, the Gospel combines the themes of judgment and deliverance. This is also the case when the good news of Jesus Christ is preached. Here the realities of the New Covenant (i.e., the unsearchable riches of Christ that we preach) are always proclaimed against the background of human depravity and rebellion — a predicament that must be overcome by the gracious reign of God in Christ Jesus.

Based upon these insights, Frank Stagg defines the Gospel as:

"The good news that God has come in his power to establish his kingdom, bringing evil under his judgment, overcoming forces hostile to himself, and offering deliverance to all who will receive it. The gospel is both judgment and promise."[1]

This general definition is supplemented by the following statement.

THE GOSPEL

The true essence of the Gospel is that our holy, loving Creator, confronted with human hostility and rebellion, has chosen in His own freedom and faithfulness to become our holy, loving Redeemer and Restorer. The Father has sent the Son to be the Savior of the world (I John 4:14); it is through His one of a kind Son that God's plan of salvation is implemented. So Peter announced: *Salvation is found in no one else, for there is no other name under heaven given to men by which we must be saved*" (Acts 4:12). And Christ Himself taught: "I am the way, the truth and the life. No one comes to the Father except through me" (John 14:6).

Through the Gospel we learn that, we human beings, who were made for fellowship with God, are by nature unresponsive to, and separated from, our Maker. We are constantly twisting His truth, breaking His law, belittling His goals and standards and offending His holiness by our unholiness, so that we truly are "without hope and without God in the world" (Romans 1:18-32; 3:9-20; Ephesians 2:1-3, 12). Yet God, in His grace, took the initiative to reconcile us to Himself through the sinless life and vicarious death of his beloved Son (Ephesians 2:4-10; Romans 3:21-24).

The Father sent the Son to liberate us from the dominion of sin and Satan, and to make us His very own children and friends. Jesus paid our penalty, in our place, on His cross, thus satisfying the demands of divine justice by shedding His blood in sacrifice and so making possible justification for all who trust in Him (Romans 3:25-26). The Bible describes this mighty subsitutionary transaction as the achieving of ransom, reconciliation, redemption, propitiation, and conquest of evil powers (Matthew 20:28; 2 Corinthians 5:18-21; Romans 3:23-25; John 12:31; Colossians 2:15). It secures for us a restored relationship with God that brings pardon and peace, acceptance and access, and adoption into God's family (Colossians 1:20; 2:13-14; Romans 5:1-2; Galatians 4:4-7; I Peter 3:18).

This Gospel further proclaims the bodily resurrection, ascension, and enthronement of Jesus as evidence of the saving power of His once-for-all sacrifice for us, of the reality of His present personal ministry to us, and of the certainty of His future return to glorify us (I Corinthians 15; Hebrews 1:1-4; 2:1-18; 4:14-16; 7:1-10:25). In the life of faith, as the Gospel presents it, believers are united with their risen Lord, communing with Him, and looking to Him in repentance and hope for empowering through the Holy Spirit, so that henceforth they may not sin but serve Him truly.

God's justification of those who trust Him, according to the Gospel, is a decisive transition, here and now, from a state of condemnation and wrath, because of their sins, to one of acceptance and favor by virtue of Jesus flawless obedience, culminating in His voluntary sin-bearing death. God "justifies the wicked" (ungodly: Romans 4:5) by imputing (reckoning, crediting, counting, accounting) righteousness to them and ceasing to count their sins against them (Romans 4:1-8). Sinners receive, through faith in Christ alone, "the gift of righteousness" (Romans 1:17; 5:17; Philippians 3:9) and thus become "the righteousness of God" in Him who was made sin" for them (2 Corinthians 5:21).

As our sins were reckoned to Christ, so Christ's righteousness is reckoned to us. This is justification by the imputation of Christ's righteousness. All we bring to the transaction is our need of it. Our faith in the God who bestows it is itself the fruit of God's grace. Faith links us vitaly to Jesus, but not in a meritorious fashion.

The Gospel assures us that all who have entrusted their lives to Jesus Christ are born again children of God (John 1:12), indwelt by the Holy Spirit (Romans 7:6; 8:9-17). The moment we truly believe in Christ, the Father declares us righteous in Him and begins conforming us to His likeness. Genuine faith acknowledges and depends upon Jesus as Lord and expresses itself in growing obedience to the Word of God. All of this however, contributes nothing to the ground of our basic justification (James 2:14-26; Hebrews 6:1-12).

All believers are entitled to, and should earnestly seek, the promise of the Father, the Baptism in the Holy Spirit, according to the command of our Lord Jesus Christ. This was the normal experience of all in the earliest Christian communities. With it comes the enduement of power for life and service, the bestowment of the gifts and their uses in the work of the ministry (Luke 24:49; Acts 1:4, 8; I Corinthians 12:1-31). This experience is distinct from, and subsequent to, the experience of the new birth (Acts 8:12-17; 10:44-46; 11:14-16; 15:7-9). With the Baptism in the Holy Spirit come such experience as an overflowing fullness of the Spirit (John 7:37-39; Acts 4:8), a deepened reverence for God (Acts 2:43; Hebrews 12:28), an intensified consecration to God and dedication to His work (Acts 2:42), and a more active love for Christ, for His Word, and for the lost (Mark 16:20).

By his sanctifying grace, Christ works within us through faith, leading us to real maturity, that measure of development which is meant "by the fullness of Christ" (Ephesians 4:13). The Gospel calls us to live as obedient servants of Christ and as His representatives in the world, doing justice, loving mercy, and helping all in need, thus seeking to bear witness to the Kingdom of Christ. At death, Christ takes the believer to himself (Philippians 1:21) for unimaginable joy in the ceaseless worship of God (Revelation 22:1-5).

Salvation in its full sense is from the guilt of sin in the past, the power of sin in the present, and the presence of sin in the future. Thus, while in foretaste believers enjoy salvation now, they still await salvation in its fullness (Mark 14:61-62; Hebrews 9:28). Salvation is a Trinitarian reality, initiated by the Father, implemented by the Son, and applied by the Holy Spirit. It has a global dimension, for God's plan is to save believers out of every tribe and tongue (Revelation 5:9) to be His church, the new humanity, the people of God, the body and bride of Christ, and the community of the Holy Spirit. All the heirs of final salvation are called here and now to serve their Lord and each other in love, to share in the fellowship of Jesus sufferings, and to work together to make Christ known to the whole world.

We learn from the Gospel that, as all have sinned, so all who do not receive Christ will be judged according to their just desserts as measured by God's holy law, and will face eternal retributive punishment.[2]

CALLED TO PREACH

Contrary to popular opinion, every born-again believer has an obligation to preach this Gospel everywhere (Acts 8:1-4). It is by the anointed preaching of the "Good news" that the Holy Spirit calls and invites men, women and children to come to Jesus Christ, and offers them the "riches of His grace." Note the following key points concerning the Gospel invitation and offer:

1. It is free to every "sin-sick" person who needs God's grace and forgiveness (Isa. 55:1)

2. It is universal (Mk. 16:15).

3. It is sincerely extended (Mt. 23:37).

Now, you need to understand that, in spite of your sincerity and zeal in preaching the Gospel of the Kingdom, the Gospel does not always produce the desired effect in the hearts of those who hear it. The New Testament Scriptures suggest at least three reasons why this is so:

1. The perverse will of man is probably the main reason why the Word doesn't automatically produce positive results (Acts 7:51).

2. In His teachings about the Sower and the Seed, Jesus suggests that the condition of the heart affects the productivity of the Word (Mt. 13:1-9, 18-23).

3. The Apostle James reveals that filthiness and wickedness must be laid aside if the Word is going to work for us. (Jas. 1:20-25).

So get rid of all uncleanness and the rampant outgrowth of wickedness, and in a humble (gentle, modest) spirit receive and welcome the Word which implanted and rooted (in your hearts) contains the power to save your souls.

James 1:21 AMP

Conclusion

Thus, we reiterate that in the last days, God will raise up and release into this terminal generation an elite cadre of preachers who will proclaim the Good News about God and His Rule of righteousness, peace and joy in the Holy Spirit. In the midst of unrest and upheaval, yea, amid the very spirit of the anti-Christ, the truth about God's provision in and through the shed blood of Jesus Christ will ring out. Many men, women and children will hear this message and believe it and fulfill its demands. Many will reject it, to their detriment. But, to as many as receive Him (Jesus Christ) to them is given the right to become members of the redeemed community of the Lord's people.

FOOD FOR THOUGHT AND DISCUSSION

What do you think of this statement by Delwin Brown? In your own words explain what he is actually saying.

The Biblical revelation of the reign of God should form the core of a Progressive Christian conception of salvation. Seeking salvation means seeking the healthful fullness of all the creation. Salvation comes into being (drawing on the messianic rather than the apocalyptic model) through this-worldly processes of nature, history, interpersonal relationships, and the dynamics of our individual lives. The reign of God, salvation, is always future, but equally it is always a future that is already breaking into our midst.

There is real salvation in this life. Furthermore, it is fully salvation, not some temporary or stopgap measure until a better "solution" for healing comes along. It is already breaking in upon us in the variety of ways that we celebrate and cherish: a request for forgiveness, change of heart, a growth in love, a dedication to values beyond the self. It is coming among us in the father's nurturing love of his infant, the pastor's visionary leadership of her congregation, the educator's insightful exposure of racism, the corporate executive's insistence on fair employment practices, the labor leader's work on behalf of living wages, and the citizen's defense of a sustainable environment. It comes near to us in legislative action that curbs bigotry, extends freedom, improves education, provides health care, encourages economic equality, recognizes the integrity of all the creation and promises its well-being.

These (like Jesus' treatment of the Samaritan woman, his healing of the sick, his ministry among the outcast, his overturning the tables of the money changers, and his assurance of forgiveness) are genuine "in-breakings" of salvation. In them and through them the incarnate God is working. Salvation, viewed from the perspective of the reign of God, is the process of bringing the creation, at any point and anytime, toward the fulfillment and healthful community that is envisioned in the ideal of the two great commandments. [3]

Appendix (A)

The Significance of Jesus

Christianity has a center. It is Jesus Christ. Among other things, this means that, it is impossible for us to talk about God, salvation, or worship without including Jesus in the conversation. In the NT, Jesus is the key to understanding the nature, character and ultimate intentions of God. He is the very ground of salvation and is worshipped as the risen and exalted Lord and Savior of the world. Indeed, Jesus is the true center of our Christian faith.

The Hebrew word "yeshua" and the Arabic word" "Isa" literally means "God saves." This is the name suggested by the angel Gabriel in Matthew 1:21. The Word "Christ" is really a title (not a last name). Again, in the Hebrew, the term "Messiah" parallels the Greek word "Christ" and refers to a person who has been raised up by God for some specific purpose. The general belief was (in Biblical times) that, the Messiah would be king, a new King, likened unto David of old. He would, in a very real and definitive sense, open up a glorious new era in the history of the chosen people of God. They called it, the age of the Messiah. Israel looked, with mixed expectations, for the coming of this "Messianic Age." This is seen in the background of the gospel accounts of the ministry of Jesus. It is against this background that Jesus emerges, not as just another Hamitic Jew, but, as the promised Savior and liberator spoken of by the prophets. Those who encountered Him (and received Him by faith) called Him "Immanuel" and obtained, thereby the right to be called the children of God (Jn. 1:12-13).

The NT moreover reveals something of the Person or identity of Jesus through such additional titles as "LORD" (Greek "KURIOS") and "SON of GOD." In the NT, Lord is a polite title of respect when addressing a man of substance. (see Martha's conversation with Jesus in John 11:21.)

Yet another way "Lord" is used can be seen in Romans 10:9 and I Corinthians 12:3. Here, the apostle Paul regarded the confession "Jesus is Lord" as a declaration of the main ingredient in the Gospel message. To qualify as an authentic Christian, one must "call upon the Name of the Lord" (Romans 10:13). One must invoke or call upon Jesus as "God with us." Thus, "LORD" is used here (as elsewhere in the Scriptures) to identify a divine being (or perhaps at the very least a person who is decidedly more than a mere human).

Well over 6000 times in the Bible, the sacred name of God is translated by the word "Lord." Interestingly, the writers of the NT, in particular, had no problem using this name in reference to Jesus. Notwithstanding the fact that, the Jews used this name exclusively to refer to God, the Holy Spirit inspired ministers of the New Covenant deliberately (that is with informed intentionality) made the revolutionary identification of God and the person of Jesus Christ. Indeed, Jesus had been raised from the dead by the glory of the Father, and seated at the right hand of the majesty on high where He reigns now as the mediatorial Lord of lords and King of kings (Phil. 2:10-11).

Jesus is also referred to in the NT as the "Son of God." This revelation is solidly embedded in the Biblical traditions. The wider witness of the NT builds on this revelation by distinguishing Jesus ("The only begotten Son of God") and all born again believers (the adopted sons of God). The apostolic claim is that, there is something unique about the relationship between Jesus and God the Father, as is expressed in the title "Son of God." Jesus, in addressing God as "Abba", indicated that He enjoyed a very intimate (filial) relationships with God that was unparalleled anywhere in the universe.

The apostle John alluded to this special Father-Son relationship when he called Jesus "the only one of-a-kind" Son (Jn. 3:16). The African elder, Arius, and his followers missed it, and so also did Joseph Smith and the Church of Jesus Christ of Latter Day Saints. God is not the Father of our Lord in any physical sense. In other words, God the Father **did not** have sex with the virgin Mary (as Joseph Smith taught). To insist on this is to be guilty of what Muslims call the hersy of "ittakhadha." The Biblical sense of "Son of God' is that, Jesus [as the bearer of this title] is the unique source of divine revelation and the true agent of the salvation which is from God.

Finally, the radical witness of the NT to the person of Jesus Christ climaxes with the equally radical declaration that, **Jesus is God**. At this point in our study, it is imperative that the following texts be read in several translations and versions:

John 1:1, 18; 20:28, "My Lord and my God"

Romans 9:5, "the Christ who is God over all"

Titus 2:13, "Our great God and Savior Jesus Christ"

Hebrews 1:8-9, "Your throne, O God"

II Peter 1:1, "Our God and Savior Jesus Christ"

I John 5:20, "He is the true God and eternal life"

See also these additional references that strongly suggest the same conclusion: Matthew 1:23; John 17:3; Galatians 2:20; Ephesians 5:5; Colossians 2:2; II Thessalonians 1:12 and I Timothy 3:16.

The bottom line in all of this is that, Jesus, our Messiah, is exactly who and what He is revealed to be in the Holy Scriptures. **He is the revealer of God** (Colossians 1:15; Hebrews 1:3). Two major voices from the history of the Christian church are worth listening to at this point:

> God does not want to be known except through Christ; nor can he be known in any other way. Christ is the offspring promised to Abraham; on him God has grounded all his promises. Therefore, Christ alone is the means, the life, and the mirror through which we see God and know his will. Through Christ, God declares his favor and mercy to us. In Christ we see that God is not an angry master and judge but a gracious and kind father, who blesses us, that is, who delivers us from the law, sin, death, and every evil, and gives us righteousness and eternal life through Christ. This is a certain and true knowledge of God and divine persuasion, which does not fail, but depicts God himself in a specific form, apart from which there is no God.
>
> —Martin Luther

> When Holy Scripture speaks of God, it does not permit us to let our attention or thoughts wander at random … When Holy Scripture speaks of God, it concentrates our attention and thoughts upon one single point and what is to be known at that point… If we ask further concerning the one point upon which, according to Scripture, our attention and

thoughts should and must be concentrated, then from first to last the Bible directs us to the name of Jesus Christ.

—Swiss Theologian Karl Barth

The idea here is that, in the person of Jesus Christ, God has actually stepped into the world of space and time. Moreover, it is upon this truth that the Christian church has historically believed that Jesus Christ provides a real "window into God" that is truly life-changing and gracious.

Last, but certainly not least, Jesus is revealed in sacred Scripture as **the "Savior, who is Christ the Lord"** (Luke 2:11). **He came to give His life as a ransom for many** (Mark 10:45; I Timothy 2:5-6). In other words, Jesus gave his life to achieve liberation for those held captive by sin. He moreover saves by redeeming and reconciling individuals who are in "the wrong place "and "wrong condition" (Galatians 3:13; 4:5; II Corinthians 5:19).

So, how significant is Jesus? And, what kind of value should we place upon Him? For the NT writers Jesus Christ, through His life, death and resurrection, has opened up a world of lifesaving possibilities for any person who will receive Him by faith. There is no salvation without Him! He is the revealed Way, Truth, and Life, and no one can make it to the Father by rejecting His "only begotten Son."

Perhaps the apostle Paul says it best. In speaking of "God's dear Son," he clearly establishes the fact that, Jesus is the center of our faith.

In whom we have redemption through his blood even the forgiveness of sins. Who is the image of the invisible God, the firstborn of every creature: For by him were all things created, that are in heaven, and that are in earth, visible and invisible, whether they be thrones, or dominions, or principalities or powers: all things were created by him, and for him: And he is before all things, and by him all things consist. And he is the head of the body, the church; who is the beginning, the firstborn from the dead; that in all things he might have the preeminence. For it pleased the Father that in him should all fullness dwell; And, having made peace through the blood of his cross, by him to reconcile all things unto himself,' by him I say, whether they be things in earth, or things in heaven.

For me, and other modern-day Christians, the significance of Jesus may be summarized by simply saying,

"He is my all in all."

Appendix (B)

The Jesus Creed/Credo
This Creed was originally shared
At the Emergent Convention, Nashville, May 2004

I. We have confidence in Jesus
    Who healed the sick, the blind, and the paralyzed.
    And even raised the dead.

    He cast out evil powers and
    Confronted corrupt leaders.
    He cleansed the temple.
    He favored the poor.
    He turned water into wine.
    Walked on water, calmed storms.

    He died for the sins of the world,
    Rose from the dead, and ascended to the Father.
    Sent the Holy Spirit.

II. We have confidence in Jesus
    Who taught in word and example,
    Signs and wonders.
    He preached parables of the Kingdom of God
    On hillsides, from boats, in the temple, in homes,
    At banquets and parties, along the road, on beaches, in towns,
    By day and night.

    He taught the way of love for God and neighbor,
    For stranger and enemy, for outcast and alien.

III. We have confidence in Jesus,
Who called disciples, led them,
Gave them new names and new purpose.
And sent them out to preach good news.
He washed their feet as a servant.
He walked with them, ate with them,
Called them friends,
Rebuked them, encouraged them,
Promised to leave and then return,
And promised to be with them always.

He taught them to pray.
He rose early to pray, stole away to desolate places,
Fasted and faced agonizing temptations,
Wept in a garden,
And prayed, "not my will but your will be done."
He rejoiced, he sang, he feasted, he wept.

IV. We have confidence in Jesus,
So we follow him, learn his ways,
Seek to obey his teaching and live by his example.
We walk with him, walk in him, abide in him,
As a branch in a vine.
We have not seen him, but we love him.
His words are to us words of life eternal,
And to know him is to know the true and living God.
We do not see him now, but we have confidence in Jesus.
Amen.

Appendix (C)

The Exchange at Calvary

Borne by Christ	Benefit to the Believer
1.OUR TRANSGRESSIONS AND INIQUITIES (Isa. 53:5)	1.PEACE i.e. forgiveness and reconciliation (Rom. 5:10; Eph. 2:14-17)
2.OUR GRIEFS (sickness) AND SORROWS (pains) (Isa. 53:5)	2.HEALING FOR THE PHYSICAL BODY (I Pet. 2:24)
3.GUILT, SIN NOTE! Jesus was made the offering for sin. (Isa. 53:4-5)	3.RIGHTEOUSNESS (II Cor. 5:21)
4.OUR "SINFULNESS" (Micah 6:13); See also Isa. 1:5-6; 52:13-15 re: Jesus' suffering on the cross.	4.PERFECT SOUNDNESS THROUGH HIS NAME (Acts 3:16)

Borne by Christ	Benefit to the Believer
5.THE CURSE OF THE LAW – unfruitfulness, insufficiency, frustration, failure, defeat, bondage, fear, sickness (Gal. 3:13-14; Dt. 28:16-68)	5.THE BLESSINGS OF ABRAHAM – fruitfulness, abundance, protection, direction, victory, success, holiness, dominion, and riches. (Dt. 28:2-13)
6.POVERTY: Jesus endured hunger, thirst, nakedness and want of all things on the cross. (Dt. 28:47-48; II Cor. 8:9)	6.RICHES, WEALTH (Jn. 10:10; II Cor. 8:9)

7.DEATH Heb. 2:9; Mt. 27:46 ff. I Pet. 3:18-19)	7.LIFE i.e., union and fellowship with God now; plus, eternity in God's presence (I Cor. 6:17; 15:51-54)
8.OUR OLD MAN EXE-CUTED (Rom. 6:6)	8.NEW MAN BROUGHT FORTH (Eph. 4:24)

Appendix (D)

Is the New Covenant for Israel or the Church?

November 6, 2014 By: Sam Storms

In Hebrews 8 the author of that epistle cites Jeremiah 31 regarding the New Covenant. There God spoke through the OT prophet and said, "Behold, the days are coming, declares the Lord, when I will establish a new covenant with the house of Israel and with the house of Judah" (Heb. 8:8b).

But wouldn't that mean that we, the Church of Jesus Christ, have no membership in this covenant and can't benefit from its blessings? After all, most of us are Gentiles and have not descended physically from Israel or Judah. No, it means no such thing!

This is a huge theological question that I can only address briefly. So let me say just a couple of things. The church is comprised of believing Jews and Gentiles….

First, when the apostle Paul quotes the words of Jesus in I Corinthians 11 and tells the **Church** about its responsibility to celebrate the Lord's Supper he explicitly mentions that this is the New Covenant prophesied in Jeremiah 31. That makes no sense unless Jeremiah's prophecy is applicable to the entire Body of Christ, the entire Church, which is comprised of both believing Jews and believing Gentiles.

Second, in 2 Corinthians 3:6 Paul explicitly says that **we** are the recipients of and ministers of the New Covenant.

Third, the blessings of the prophesied New Covenant, those described in Hebrews 8 and throughout the rest of the NT, are identical with the blessings that Christians in the Church receive and enjoy; forgiveness of sins, the empowering ministry of the Holy Spirit, and the knowledge of God inscribed on our hearts.

Fourth, the people to whom the book of Hebrews was written are members of the **Church!** His point in this epistle is, "You now are participants in the new and better covenant promised in Jeremiah 31 and established by Jesus through his death and resurrection; so why would you ever want to go back under the old covenant and its inferior ways?" If the members of the church in Rome, to which this letter was addressed, are not also members of the New Covenant, nothing in this entire book makes any sense at all.

Fifth, according to Hebrews 8:6, the new covenant "is" better (present tense) and "has been enacted" (prefect tense) on better promises. And those better promises are precisely what he describes in Hebrews 8:10-15. Our author says that the Holy Spirit bears witness to **"us,"** the Church, that God has made this new covenant with us!

Seventh, you should keep in mind a couple of things about the reference to the "house of Israel" and the "house of Judah" in Hebrew 8:8.

For one thing, who was present in the upper room when Jesus inaugurated the new covenant and established the Lord Supper as the ordinance by which we celebrate it? Jews! The only people present were the disciples and their close friends, all members of either the house of Israel or Judah. Furthermore, according to Galatians 3:16 and 3:28-29 (and numerous other texts) anyone who believes in Jesus Christ is now the "seed" of Abraham and thus an heir according to the promise. In other words, the Church of Jesus Christ is the true Israel of God.

That doesn't mean believing Jews are excluded or replaced as heirs of the promise made to Abraham. All ethnic Jews who believe in Jesus are members of the New Covenant. But so too are ethnic Gentiles who believe in Jesus.

The blood in your veins no longer matters for anything. The only thing that matters is the faith in your heart: if you trust in Jesus, whether you are male or female, slave or free, Jew or Gentile, you are the seed of Abraham, the true Israel of God, and thus members of the New Covenant.

Appendix (E)

The Surpassing Glory of the New Covenant
(2 Cor. 3:4-11)

By: Sam Storms

Nothing is more frustrating than knowing what one ought to do and lacking the power to perform it. To see and read and be confronted with the will of God all the while one is bereft of the resolve and spiritual energy to respond in a positive fashion is my definition of despair!

That is why I thank God daily that I do not live in an age when the law of God was merely written on stone and called for my obedience without the promise of the provision of power. That is why I thank God daily that I have, by grace, been made a member of the New Covenant in Christ Jesus, the distinguishing feature of which is that for every precept there is power and for every statute there is strength and for the otherwise impossible task of saying yes to God's commands there is the indwelling presence of the Holy Spirit.

In describing this New Covenant of which we've been made members, Paul contrasts it with the Mosaic or Old Covenant. He associated the New with the Spirit and says that it "gives life," whereas the Old he describes as "the letter [which] kills" (2 Cor. 3:6).

This contrast has been misunderstood. It does not mean that the Law of Moses is sinful (cf. Rom. 7:12-14), nor does it allude to two ways of interpreting Scripture: literal vs. spiritual (or allegorical). Far less does it have reference to the distinction many make between *doctrine* and *spirit* or between *mind* and *heart*.

The contrast in view becomes evident when one examines the nature of the New Covenant as over against the Old. In sum, the Law of Moses was imposed from without on a rebellious people, the result of which was death. The New Covenant, on the other hand, is inscribed on the very hearts of its recipients, all of whom, from least to the greatest, will "know the Lord" (Jer. 31:33-34). All participants in the New Covenant are provided with the inner power, i.e., the Holy Spirit, to fulfill its dictates. The Old Covenant made no such provision. Its dictates confronted a people whose hearts were stone. The effect of God's commandments on unchanged (stony) hearts is condemnation and death. Thus, spiritually speaking, the Old Covenant "killed" and made it, therefore, "a ministry of death" (v. 7a).

Scott Hafemann provides this excellent summation of Paul's point:

"The problem with the Sinai covenant was not with the law itself, but, as Ezekiel and Jeremiah testify, with the people whose hearts remained hardened under it. The law remains for Paul, as it did for the Jewish traditions of his day, the holy, just, and good expression of God's covenantal will (Rom. 7:12). Indeed, Paul characterizes the law itself as 'spiritual'(7:14). As the expression of God's abiding will, it is not the law as 'letter.' Devoid of God's Spirit, the law remains to those who encounter it merely a rejected declaration of God's saving purposes and promises, including its corresponding calls for repentance and the obedience of faith. Although the law declares God's will, it is powerless to enable people to keep it" (132).

Thus the inadequacy of the Mosaic Law was not due to any inherent sinfulness or failure on its part. Its inadequacy, rather, was that it could only *prescribe* what people ought to do but *without making provision* that would sufficiently enable them to fulfill its commands. The Law of Moses was quite effective in explaining one's moral obligation and exposing one's sin, but it was not endowed with the power to ensure that those who stood under its covenant would fulfill its terms.

That there should be no doubt concerning the inherent goodness of the Old Covenant established through Moses, Paul himself speaks of its "glory" no fewer than six times in vv. 7-11, and no fewer than four times refers to the superior "glory" of the New Covenant established through Christ!

Before I go any further, let me say a few brief words about the New Covenant. By the way, this is no theological diversion or meaningless bunny-trail. This is the foundation for your relationship with God! Nothing could be more personal or important than understanding the terms on which we relate to God as our Lord and Savior and experience the blessings he has provided.

First of all, what is provided for us in the *New Covenant?* According to what we read in Jeremiah 31:31-34 (cf. Ezek. 36:25-28) it entails several glorious blessings, such as *the internalization of God's law* ("I will put my law within them, and I will write it on their hearts, " Jer. 31:33a; cf. 2 Cor. 3:3), *unbroken fellowship with God* ("I will be their God, and they shall be my people," Jer. 31:33b), *unmediated knowledge of God* ("And they shall all know me, from the least of them to the greatest, declares the Lord," Jer. 33:34a), and *the unconditional forgiveness of sins* ("for I will forgive their iniquity, and I will remember their sin no more," Jer. 33:34b).

Second, *in whom* is the New Covenant *fulfilled?* I'm always a bit stunned that anyone could have any doubts about this, but let me briefly mention five answers that have been given.

Some so-called "classical dispensationalists" argue that the New Covenant was given exclusively for ethnic Israel and will therefore be fulfilled only in her at the end of the age when Israel as a nation is saved. The Church according to this view, has no part in the blessings of this covenant.

There have been other dispensationalists who argued that there are two New Covenants, one for ethnic Israel, in which the Church shares *spiritually.* In other words, those blessings in the covenant which pertain to salvation are equally enjoyed by the Church, but those that pertain to *earthly prominence in the land* belong solely to Israel.

A fourth view, not very popular but extremely unbiblical and dangerous, is that there are two covenants, one for the Jewish people and one for those (whether Jew or Gentile) who embrace Jesus as Messiah. The latter comprise the Church. The former are Jews who need *not* believe that Jesus is the Messiah but who relate savingly to God via Judaism and the covenant God uniquely established with them as a nation.

The correct view, in my opinion, is that there is only one New Covenant. The Church, being the historical continuation of the believing remnant within Israel, is the recipient of its blessings. Thus, both believing Jews and believing Gentiles, the latter of whom have been graciously included in the covenants of promise (Eph. 2:12), together, and equally, enjoy the fulfillment of all aspects of the New Covenant (see especially Mt. 26:28; Mark 14:24; Luke 22:20; I Cor. 11:25; 2 Cor. 3:6; Gal. 3:29; Eph. 2:11-22; 3:6; Hebrews 8:6-13; 9:15; 10:15; 10:19ff.).

It is as a minister of this New Covenant that Paul happily declares he has been made adequate or sufficient *by God*. He finds nothing in himself that would qualify him for this awesome task. God made him "competent" (v. 5), as is surely the case with each of us in the exercise of any spiritual gift or ministry or act of service to which God has called us.

What a blessing indeed, that the superior glory of the "ministry of the Spirit" (v. 8) or the "ministry of righteousness" (v. 9), i.e., the ministry of the New Covenant, will never fade away or be abolished or replaced by one that surpasses it in power or preeminence (v. 11). For its provisions we give thanks and on its power we rely as we seek to live to the glory of its Giver.

Sam

ENDNOTES

Chapter One: "The New Covenant"
I would strongly recommend (as a collateral resource) the book by Kevin Conner and Ken Malmin entitled, **"The Covenants"** (Portland, Oregon, City Christian Publishing, 1983), 69-91

Chapter Two: Jesus Christ: God & Man
[1] Dr. Walter McCray, *The Black Presence in the Bible* (Black Light Fellowship, Chicago, II) p. 125-129. See also, the chapter entitled, "The Black Messiah" in Black theology, a Documentary History, Volume One.
[2] The doctrine of the Immaculate Conception of Mary is the belief that Mary, as the mother of Jesus, was conceived without any taint of sin. Our forefathers regarded this belief as lacking in Scriptural support and so, they discarded it.
[3] The effect of Adam's sin on the human race is called, "Original sin." Thus all children brought into this world are naturally blighted by the inclination to sin.
[4] Charles Ryrie, *Basic Theology,* (Victor Books, Wheaton, IL) p. 260-262

Chapter Three: "Unlimited Atonement"
[1] The Bible contrasts our new life "in Christ" with our old life "in Adam." That old life was characterized by disobedience, sin, guilt, condemnation and death. "Our new life in Christ" is characterized by "Spiritual blessings" such as salvation, abundant grace, righteousness, eternal life, and the fullness of the Spirit (cp. Rom. 5:12-21; 6:8; 14:17-19; I Cor. 15:21-22, 45-49; Phil. 2:1-5; 4:6-9).
[2] Charles M. Horne, *Salvation* (Chicago, Ill. Moody Press 1971), p. 36-37. See also Leon Morris, *The Apostolic Preaching of the Cross* (Grand Rapids MI Eerdmans, 1955), p. 125-185 and John J. Murray, *Redemp-*

tion: Accomplished and Applied (Grand Rapids, MI,. Eerdmans, 1955), p. 35-39

[3] See the article entitled "The Passover" in the *Full Life Study Bible,* p. 110-111

[4] Clark H. Pinnock, *Grace Unlimited* (Minneapolis Minnesota, Bethany House Publishers, 1975), p. 21-30 "God's Universal Salvific Grace" by Vermon C. Grounds. For an insightful particularist perspective, see *Concise Theology* by J. I Packer, (Tyndale Publishers, Wheaton IL., p. 146-153. A balancing point of view may be found in Daniel balancing point of view may be found in Daniel Pocota's article entitled, "the Saving Work of Christ" in Stanley Horton's *Systematic Theology,* Logion Press, Springfield, MO.,) p. 325-373.

[5] H.C. Thiessen, Lectures in Systematic Theology. (Logion Press, Springfield, MO.,) p. 325-373.

[6] A. H. Strong, *Systematic Theology,* Valley Forge, PA. Judson Press, 1985), p. 772.

[7] Derek Prince, *Atonement, Your Appointment With God* (Grand Rapids, MI., Baker House, 2000) p. 45-132

Chapter Four: "The Benefits of The Atonement"

[1] The Hebrew word for "benefits" in Ps. 103 means "to treat a person" (well or ill), "to ripen", "to deal bountifully with," "to recompense or to reward." See *Strongs Concordance, Hebrew and Chaldee Dictionary,* #'s 1576, 1580, and 8408.

[2] Iniquities are inborn weaknesses or tendencies toward certain kinds of sin. These can usually be traced back to the sins of the forefathers (Eph. 2:3; Rom. 5:12). Patricia Beall Gruits, *Understanding God and His Covenants* (Rochester Mt. Peter Pat Publishers, 1985), p. 65-72 says, "Continuous, willful violation of the moral law of God gives rise to iniquities."

[3] John MacArthur, *Body Dynamics* (formerly *The Church, The Body of Christ*) Wheaton, IL, Victor Books, 1982 p. 33-48.

[4] IBID p. 48

[5] Adapted from chapter 3 in *Body Dynamics* by John MacArthur, Jr.

Chapter Five: "The Present-Day Ministry of Jesus Christ"

[1] Christ's present role in glory is often referred to as His "heavenly session." His present authority is expressed by saying that, he sits at the Father's right hand, not to rest but, to rule as King, and to minister as a priest.

[2] Charles Hodge, Systematic Theology, Vol. II, p. 635

[3] Kevin J Conner, *The Church in the New Testament,* p. 214-215

Chapter Six: "The Gospel of The Kingdom"

[1] Frank Stagg, **New Testament Theology** (Nashville, Tennessee, Broadman Press, 1962), p. 270-273

[2] J. I. Packer and Thomas C. Oden, **One Faith, The Evangelical Consensus** (Downers Grove, Ill. Intervarsity Press, 2004), p. 187-190

[3] Delwin Brown, **What Does A Progressive Christian Believe?** (New York, NY. Church Publishing Inc., 2008), p. 88-89

54942341R00060

Made in the USA
Middletown, DE
14 July 2019